The Nations in PROPHECY

The Nations in
PROPHECY

by
JOHN F. WALVOORD
President, Dallas Theological Seminary

792

ZONDERVAN PUBLISHING HOUSE
Grand Rapids, Michigan

PREFACE

The story of man as told in history and prophecy is the most exciting drama ever written. It is the story of the omnipotent God unfolding His purpose for the nations in measured movements designed to demonstrate His own sovereignty, wisdom, and power. In the original creation, man was made in the image and likeness of God. In the fall, that image was marred, but man nevertheless was destined to be the channel of divine revelation. The history of the race was designed, on the one hand, to demonstrate the inadequacy of the creature, and, on the other, the sufficiency of the omnipotent Creator. Earth was to be the divine stage and man the actor, but there can be no question that human destiny remains in the hands of the unseen God, even if at times He seems to work behind the scenes.

In the development of the divine purpose in history in the Old Testament, God chose Israel to be the principal actor and, using this vehicle of divine revelation, God demonstrated His righteousness, faithfulness, and love. In the New Testament God revealed His plan for the church, composed of Jew and Gentile alike who would receive by faith the Son of God. In the church God supremely demonstrated His marvelous grace. In the background of these two major movements of God are the nations of the world. Israel had to deal with these nations in the Old Testament, and from these nations would come the Gentile believers to be incorporated into the church of the New Testament.

Amazingly little attention has been paid to the sovereign dealings of God with the nations. Although many have written on Israel and the church, the author does not know of any volume which attempts to do precisely what has been undertaken here, namely, to make a compilation, necessarily in summary form, of history and prophecy as it relates to the nations of the world. The study of this major theme of prophecy is richly rewarding. In no other theme of Scripture is it so evident that God is the God of history and that human history is His story.

The atmosphere of divine dealings with the nations is captured succinctly in the dramatic opening of the second Psalm where the question is raised, "Why do the heathen rage, and the people imagine a vain thing?" The psalmist describes the scene, "The kings of the earth set themselves, and the rulers take counsel together, against the LORD, and against his anointed, saying, Let us break their bands asunder, and cast away their cords from us" (Psalm 2:2, 3). At this rebellion of the nations against God, so childish and characteristic of the creature, the psalmist records the reaction of God, "He that sitteth in the heavens shall laugh: the LORD shall have them in derision" (Psalm 2:4). Then follows the great pronouncement that it is God's purpose that His Son shall rule in Zion. In the light of this the nations are instructed, "Be wise now therefore, O ye kings: be instructed, ye judges of the earth. Serve the LORD with fear, and rejoice with trembling. Kiss the Son, lest he be angry, and ye perish from the way, when his wrath is kindled but a little. Blessed are all they that put their trust in him" (Psalm 2:10-12). The panorama of human history and prophecy is the fulfillment of this declaration of God which answers the question of the ages concerning the meaning of history.

In compiling the many technical details related to the history of nations, many standard works have been consulted. The author is especially indebted to Dr. Merrill F. Unger and Dr. Bruce K. Waltke of the Department of Semitics and Old Testament at Dallas Theological Seminary for their many helpful suggestions. Acknowledgment is also made of permission to use with revision portions of a chapter by the author in *The Prophetic Word in Crisis Days* (Dunham Publishing Company, 1961).

The study of history and prophecy as it relates to the nations is especially appropriate at this point in the twentieth century when history seems to be moving rapidly toward its destiny. Only the divine interpretation of history and the divine revelation of the prophetic future of nations can give us a sure light in these troubled days. The present divine purpose for the nations, revealed in the command to "teach all nations" (Matthew 28:19), was never more relevant or urgent than in the present hour. For those who do not hear and those who do not heed among the nations, the Scriptures are plain in their warning of divine judgment. The future will demonstrate the wisdom of the proverb, "Righteousness exalteth a nation: but sin is a reproach to any people" (Proverbs 14:34). It may be in our generation that Jesus Christ will come as King of kings and Lord of lords to judge the nations and to establish His righteous rule. Then all men "shall be blessed in him: all nations shall call him blessed" (Psalm 72:17). In that hour "all kings shall fall down before him: all nations shall serve him" (Psalm 72:11). Meanwhile, as we wait the dawn of the consummation of the ages, the invitation is still extended, "Kiss the Son," and the promise is still valid, "Blessed are all they that put their trust in him" (Psalm 2:12).

CONTENTS

The Nations in PROPHECY

CHAPTER I

THE NATIONS IN CRISIS

The world today faces an international crisis unparalleled in all the history of man. A tremendous revolution is under way in the international scene, in science, in economics, in morals, in theology, and in the religious structure of the church. The world is aflame with the raw passions of men ambitious for power and desperate to be freed from poverty and frustration. An ominous cloud hangs over the hearts of men and nations. The nations are indeed at the crossroads, and impending events cast their shadow on every aspect of human life. The world is moving faster and faster like a colossal machine out of control whose very power and momentum inevitably will plunge it into ultimate disaster.

Apart from the Bible, the world does not have a ray of hope. Our most brilliant leaders have not found an answer. World leaders, whether in Moscow or Washington, are troubled by the great issues which face the world today. President John F. Kennedy before his untimely assassination expressed the viewpoint of western civilization when he said, "I speak today in an hour of national peril, and of national opportunity. Before my term has ended, we shall have to test anew whether a nation organized and governed such as ours can endure. The outcome is by no means certain. The tide of events has been running out, and time has not been our friend."

The present world crisis is not a result of any one factor, but a concurrence of causes and effects which combine to set the world stage for a conflict which may quickly bring an end to hundreds of years of progress in western civilization and establish new centers of international power. Whatever the future holds, it is going to be dramatically different than the past. In this dark picture only the Scriptures chart a sure course and give us an intelligent explanation of world-wide confusion as it exists today. The present world crisis in the light of the Scriptures reveals the existence of remarkable components in almost every area which may lead to a dramatic climax of world history. The present crises in every area of human life all point to the same conclusion, that disaster awaits the nations of the world.

SPIRITUAL CRISIS

The twentieth century has witnessed a gathering spiritual crisis. The history of the church to some extent has paralleled the intellectual progress of the world since apostolic days. For many centuries Christianity was largely obscured in the darkness of the Middle Ages. The vigorous evangelical movement of the church largely sprang from the Protestant Reformation and political freedom which permitted the proclamation of the Gospel. During the last century an unprecedented missionary effort has been witnessed. Thousands of missionaries carried the Gospel to distant lands and the Bible was published in hundreds of tongues. Through the printed page and through radio the Gospel has reached most of the civilized world to some extent, and more individuals are within potential reach of the Gospel than ever before.

Although there are many encouraging aspects to contemporary missionary efforts, it should be obvious even to the most sanguine observer that the proclamation of the Gospel is not even keeping up with the population explosion, much less overcoming opposition engendered by the nationalism of small nations and the vigorous growth of communism in many lands. As far as numbers of converts are concerned, communism as well as some of the non-Christian religions of the world are far exceeding Christianity in its present outreach. Even in so-called Christian United States of America, Biblical truth has had realistic application to only a small segment of the population and has not materially influenced our national policies whether in politics, business, or educational areas of national activity.

The spiritual crisis is pinpointed by the rejection of Jesus Christ as Saviour and Lord by the masses of world population in every nation. In Europe, the cradle of Protestantism, only a small fraction of the total population has an intelligent belief in Jesus Christ and nowhere in the world is the Christian faith a dominant influence. It is obvious that a projection of the contemporary efforts to further the Christian faith and to introduce people to Jesus Christ will fall far short of any realistic goal. The world has plunged into an age where the great majority do not know the facts about Jesus Christ, and if they did, would probably not receive them sympathetically.

THEOLOGICAL CRISIS

If the historic Christian faith embodied in the great creeds of the church and expressed by the Protestant reformers are taken as the standards, it is evident that the church today is in a major theological crisis. Central in this controversy is the rejection of the Bible as the inerrant Word of God. In spite of the fact that more facilities are available than ever before to print, translate, and proclaim Scriptural truth, the educated people of the world have not turned to the Scriptures in faith. Within the walls of the professing church unbelief in the Scriptures has come in like a flood until many so-called Biblical scholars assume that the historic faith in the Bible as God's holy Word is now outmoded and not even worthy of debate. Substituted for Biblical faith is confidence in spiritual experience — either natural or supernatural, and in the promotion of ritualism, moralism, and rationalism.

Man has once again assumed the impossible task of defining and proclaiming infinite truth apart from God's divine revelation, an effort which history has demonstrated is doomed to failure. Churches and institutions of learning which are standing with the Protestant Reformers in fundamental doctrines are all too few and are an evident minority in the great mass of contemporary Christendom.

While in our day some of the extremes of liberalism have been rejected, there is no observable trend toward the absolute standard of accepting the Bible as the inerrant Word of God. There does not seem to be any hope of reclaiming this doctrine for the majority of the church. Organized Christendom today is like a ship without a rudder and an anchor, at the mercy of the winds of chance and bound for no certain port. The ultimate end can only be disaster for the ship and all those who put their trust in it.

MORAL CRISIS

It is only natural that spiritual crisis and theological crisis should have its ultimate end in the moral crisis of our day. Never before in the history of the world has there been more organized and deliberate immorality in defiance of Biblical ethics. The new liberal theology has bred a new morality. That such immorality should be true of the heathen world is to be expected. That it should come from cultured, educated, and liberated people is certainly an omen that only divine judgment can deal with this situation. Even in lands where Christianity has been widely taught, the basic morality of honesty and decency, the sanctity of marriage and the home, and related ethical standards are dragged into the mire of a civilization devoted to every sinful pleasure and to ridiculing any return to decency.

Such a situation is plainly treated in II Peter 2 as a natural result stemming from departure from the doctrine of the person and work of Christ. The immorality of our day is the inevitable fruit of departure from Christ and the Word of God. For it there can only be divine judgment such as the Scriptures clearly predict.

ECCLESIASTICAL CRISIS

The trend away from Biblical theology and Biblical morals has precipitated in the modern church a desire to organize all Christendom in one centrally governed body. In this way the church can achieve a powerful role in the world not dependent upon its theology or spiritual power. Although motivated in many cases by a sincere desire to advance the cause of Christ, the ecumenical movement has emerged in the modern scene as a colossus embracing all Christendom in a gigantic organization responsible to its leaders but not to its laity. This centralization of power is no substitute for the spiritual unity accomplished by the indwelling power of the Holy Spirit.

Because the majority of the organized church are committed to theological and spiritual doctrines which differ from historic Christianity, progress in the ecumenical movement can only result in the throttling of evangelical activity true to the Gospel. Both on the mission field and in the homeland its influence has tended to make the way difficult for those who still proclaim the old orthodoxy. Most important in understanding our times is the suggestion that the creation of an ecumenical church is a foreshadowing and preparation for a new world religion which in the prophetic future will be completely devoid of spiritual truth related to Christianity. The present demand for conformity to the organized church could end in the throttling of freedom of speech and conscience which would threaten any future spiritual progress for the church at large.

SCIENTIFIC CRISIS

One of the major elements in our modern world is the rapid rise of science whether in the field of electronics or the atomic structure of matter. Incredible advances are being achieved in one year which more than equal the advance in whole centuries of the past. The modern world has been brought together by rapid communication and transportation. The atomic bomb has greatly increased the ability of evil men to destroy or control. The race to command space is driven by the fear of some breakthrough which would give one nation a dominant position of power over the entire world. To the horrors of war already conceived are added the possibilities of bacteriological or chemical warfare which could well wipe out whole civilizations and drastically change the face of the earth.

The scientific colossus is such that increased knowledge brings only increased fear, and those in the best position to know have the greatest dread of that which the future may hold. The scientific advance has contributed tremendously to the accumulated evidence that the world is facing a showdown, that history in the future will not be as it was in the past, and that some gigantic crisis looms on the horizon.

RACIAL CRISIS

Among the tensions contributing to the international scene are growing racial tensions evident not only in the United States but throughout the world. It is evident that people wrongly oppressed in some cases are not content with equality and redress, but want supremacy. The down-trodden masses of the world regardless of race often find in the racial issue a springboard from which to launch their claims.

From a Biblical standpoint, antisemitism in the Middle East is a matter of major significance. The people of Israel now restored to their ancient land, although small in number, are regarded as a thorn in the side of the non-Jewish world and constitute one of the major tensions in a pivotal area of the world.

From the standpoint of prophecy this issue looms large in the present day and in the prophetic future, and Israel's restoration is by divine appointment. Israel as the chosen people is destined to a prominent place in future world affairs, but not before enduring much hardship and persecution. The racial issue, however, is not limited to the Middle East, and almost every nation under the sun has serious racial tensions on a plane never before realized in the entire history of the world.

ECONOMIC CRISIS

Those living within the United States of America have an unusual platform from which to view the economic situation of the entire world. Prosperity has swept America to a degree never before realized, and its average citizen has more money, more pleasure, more luxuries than ever before. But the United States is an island in a world of desperate economic need. Millions of the masses of the world who are oppressed and deprived of any fair share of economic wealth are clamoring to be heard. In many nations there is no middle class, but only the extremely rich and the extremely poor. The tensions raised by such a situation cannot forever lie dormant. The word *revolution* will undoubtedly be prominent in the days ahead, as oppressed people are exploited by communists as well as ambitious politicians and encouraged to rebel with empty promises of improvement in their situation.

While certain areas of the world are experiencing unprecedented prosperity, other portions are still laboring in desperate need of the basic material things of life with millions who are in constant danger of starvation and for whom the simplest shelter and provision of clothing is often lacking. The mushrooming population of the world has only aggravated the situation until major sections of the earth can no longer support themeslves. The resulting pressures inevitably will affect future world history and continue to erupt until the whole earth is caught in a world crisis combining all of these several elements.

POLITICAL CRISIS

One of the most evident areas of crisis is in the international scene with nations motivated by communistic principles attempting to wrest control from the noncommunist world. Never before in history have such dramatic changes taken place as have occurred in the last twenty-five years. During these years major countries have been freed from control of other nations and many small nations have emerged as independent states. The immaturity of the new countries and their lack of economic resources and wise leadership already have produced an erratic course which does not portend a glorious future. The world-wide struggle between communism and the noncommunist nations is moving relentlessly in favor of communism, and the question which many thoughtful leaders raise is how long will this struggle continue. For those interested in freedom of conscience, freedom of enterprise, and freedom of speech, these are indeed dark hours, and no one humanly speaking dares to predict what another generation will face.

CRISIS IN PROPHETIC FULFILLMENT

The many factors which contribute to world crisis in our day have tremendous significance as compared to the Scriptures. The amazing fact is that these factors fit into a prophetic pattern which describes the end of the age. The Bible anticipates that a world crisis would precede the coming of Christ to establish His millennial kingdom (Matthew 24:15-24). Before the final world crisis comes to its head Christ will come to take those who believe in Him out of the world in the rapture of the church (I Thessalonians 4:13 - 5:11).

In describing end-time events, the Bible makes plain that the world crisis will eventually result in a world government headed by an evil world dictator (Revelation 13:1-10). The United Nations of our present world built on the assumption that world government is the only way to world peace may well be a part of the preparation for world-wide acceptance of a world dictator as the only way out. In preparation for the formation of this world empire, the Bible seems to anticipate a revival of the ancient Roman Empire, a formation of a United States of countries in the Mediterranean area. From this will come a temporary solution of the Israel-Arab controversy by means of a covenant with the people of Israel (Daniel 9:27).

This preliminary stage, however, is only the forerunner of a final world government in which the world dictator assumes supreme control and demands that all worship him in recognition of a new world religion of which he is the head (Revelation 13:8). Israel as well as those who name the name of Christ in that day will become the objects of fearful persecution. Divine judgments in an unprecedented way will fall upon the earth (cf. Revelation 6 - 19). These and many other developments will tend to make this period a time of great tribulation. This tremendous movement will climax in a great world war and the second coming of Jesus Christ to establish His earthly kingdom.

The significance of the present world crisis is that it contains practically all the elements which are a natural preparation for the end of the age. The raging of the nations (Psalm 2:1) is the forerunner to the Son of God establishing His government in Zion (Psalm 2:6; Isaiah 2:2-4). The present generation may witness the dramatic close of the "times of the Gentiles" and the establishment of the kingdom of heaven upon the earth, thus bringing to fulfillment one of the great themes of prophecy — the divine program for the nations of the world.

Chapter II

THE BEGINNINGS OF THE NATIONS

The Beginning of Creation

The Bible is a book of beginnings. The reader of the Scriptures is introduced in the very first verse of the Bible to the sweeping statement "In the beginning God." The eternal God who knew no beginning is the source of all the beginnings which follow. In the original creation, the material universe was brought into being with all its complexity and natural law seen today in the organic and inorganic world. In this universe of mass and motion were introduced the first moral creatures, the holy angels. Each angel was the object of immediate creation. They were moral agents with moral will and intelligence capable of serving God. Some of these left their first estate in rebellion and headed by Satan became fallen angels (Isaiah 14:12-15; Ezekiel 28:12-15).

Creation of Man

The holy angels and the fallen angels, those who left their first estate, were not created in the image and likeness of God. Adam and Eve were created to fulfill this lofty purpose here on earth, and were designed to be morally like God. There is some evidence that the world of Adam and Eve was a re-creation and not the original creation of the heavens and the earth. The introduction of man, however, was something new and was the beginning of the divine purpose in which ultimately God would become man in Christ.

From Adam to Noah

The early history of man from Adam to Noah is summarized in a few short chapters which graphically picture the introduction of sin into the human race through Satanic temptation and man's choice to disobey God. The downward course of humanity was rapid. Genesis 6:5-7 depicts God observing the great wickedness

21

of man, "that every imagination of the thoughts of his heart was only evil continually," and God declared His purpose, "I will destroy man whom I have created from the face of the earth; both man, and beast, and the creeping thing, and the fowls of the air" (Genesis 6:7). The only bright spot in the unrelieved depravity of man was that "Noah found grace in the eyes of the Lord" (Genesis 6:8). Of the many thousands which populated the earth at that time only Noah and his wife and three sons and their wives were worth saving from the flood which God declared would compass the earth.

The Flood

The story of the flood must have been important in the eyes of God for more space is given to it in Genesis than the whole story of creation and more than the whole history from Adam to Noah. This was another new beginning, a wiping out of that which was spoiled and impossible of restoration, and a beginning with a godly family which, in the midst of universal corruption, had found faith and grace and manifested a determination to do the will of God. Noah lived to the ripe old age of 950 years, one of the oldest men in the Bible, exceeded only by Methuselah who lived 969 years. Most important, however, is the historic fact that Noah became the father of the entire human race. His three sons born before the flood, Japheth, Ham, and Shem were to be the progenitors of mankind subsequently born on the earth. There is no record of any other sons of Noah, and his three sons who shared with him the task of building the ark and who survived the flood were to be the means by which God repopulated the earth.

Introduction of Human Government

The new beginning with Noah and his sons also marked the progression and the unfolding of the divine purpose in human history. In Noah and his family for the first time were exercised the prerogatives of human government, the right of man to rule his fellow men. Adam had been given the charge to "subdue" the earth (Genesis 1:28), but he did not properly execute his responsibility. The commission, therefore, was renewed with enlargement to Noah in Genesis 9:1-6 embodied in the dictum, "Whoso sheddeth man's blood, by man shall his blood be shed: for in the image of God made he man" (Genesis 9:6).

The sword of divine retribution was placed in the hand of man in an attempt to control the natural lawlessness of the human heart. The principle of government thus introduced is reinforced throughout the Scriptures and is reiterated in Romans 13:1-7. In Romans the political ruler is declared to be "ordained of God" (Romans 13:1) and "the minister of God, a revenger to execute wrath upon him that doeth evil" (Romans 13:4). The human conscience proved unreliable when operating individually and thus the corporate responsibility of human government was introduced.

The place of human government in the world looms large in much of the history of the race as well as in prophecy of the end time. God has declared His concern for governments which God has recognized and with whom He is going to deal. The ultimate human government will be that of Christ Himself as He rules in the millennium and in its eternal form in the new heaven and the new earth. Earthly governments though ordained of God have largely been in rebellion against Him. As the psalmist said, "Why do the heathen rage?" and, "The kings of the earth set themselves, and the ruler take counsel together, against the LORD, and against his anointed" (Psalm 2:1, 2). God's answer is, "Yet have I set my king upon my holy hill of Zion" (Psalm 2:6).

PROPHECY CONCERNING NOAH'S SONS

Early in the history of the race prophecy begins to cast its guiding light upon the course of future human events. God promised that never again would the waters of the flood destroy all flesh (Genesis 9:15). The rainbow was made a symbol of this covenant (Genesis 9:13-17).

The most important prophecy relating to the nations which has laid the guidelines for all subsequent human history was the aftermath of a dark chapter in the life of godly Noah when he drank wine from his newly planted vineyards and became drunk (Genesis 9:20, 21). The irreverence of Ham in comparison to the respect of Shem and Japheth as they dealt with their father in his weakness led to Noah's solemn words recorded in Genesis 9:25-27, "And he said, Cursed be Canaan; a servant of servants shall he be unto his brethren. And he said, Blessed be the LORD God of Shem; and Canaan shall be his servant. God shall enlarge Japheth, and he shall dwell in the tents of Shem; and Canaan shall be his servant."

This prophetic utterance reveals that the human race would

be divided according to the natural divisions stemming from the three sons of Noah. Canaan or the descendants of Canaan, the youngest son of Ham, were to be cursed, a servile people. By contrast Shem is to be the master of Canaan and "blessed of the LORD God." It was through Shem that God's divine revelation was to come, the Scriptures were to be written, Israel to be chosen, and ultimately the Saviour and Redeemer was to appear. The contrast between Canaan and Shem is a prophetic one, not an exhortation or justification to mistreat the descendants of Ham. These broad prophecies were to characterize the people as a whole. It was not to prevent those who sought the Lord among the descendants of Ham from enjoying His blessing nor was it to assure those who were descendants of Shem that they would avoid the righteous judgment of God so largely written in God's dealings with Israel in the captivities and similar chastisements.

The immediate history that followed Noah's prophetic utterances does not constitute evidence that the curse or the blessing was necessarily immediately administered to any particular generation or individual, for many hundreds of years after Noah the descendants of Ham seemed to have flourished, and by contrast the children of Israel, the descendants of Shem, became slaves in Egypt. But, the principle laid down has subsequently been justified and constitutes God's ultimate purpose in dealing with these broad divisions of humanity.

By contrast Japheth is promised enlargement. Enlargement was not immediately evident in subsequent history of the race, but eventually the promise was fulfilled. In the history of the world since the time of Christ, the descendants of Japheth have become the principal custodians of Gentile power and have spread over the world in their power and wealth. The original prophecy indicated that Japheth would somehow inherit the blessings stemming from Shem. It has been fulfilled in that many among the Gentiles have participated in the redemption provided by Christ of the line of Shem. These original prophecies, broad in their scope and extensive in their fulfillment, will provide the framework of the history of the nations as well as the prophetic picture of that which will constitute the nations in the end of the age.

THE DESCENDANTS OF NOAH

One of the great chapters in the Bible often neglected in casual Bible study is Genesis 10, with its chronicle of the descendants of

Noah. It is obvious from the study of this chapter that here we have the background of nations which ultimately emerged and what is recorded here as history is the framework for prophecy. The compilation of the descendants of Noah is not simply a genealogy, but is designed to account for the great nations which later covered the inhabited earth.

The record of Genesis 10 is more than an ethnography, that is, a description of origin of races, but it is a profound introduction to ethnology, having to do also with the distribution, relationship, and significance of the descendants of Noah in history. Genesis 10 is one of the most remarkable historical records of this kind to be found anywhere in ancient literature, and all studies of anthropology and related sciences must begin with the facts given here. It is possible that Moses had before him documentary evidence which he used in writing the chapter, but in any case the Spirit of God guided him in selection, correction, and accurate expression of that which was far more important to subsequent history than even Moses imagined.

Broadly speaking, humanity is divided into three great divisions, that of Shem, the most important from the Biblical point of view, issuing into the Semitic family; that of Ham, sometimes referred to as the Turanian; and that of Japheth, the Aryan. That these peoples intermarried and often lived side by side in early history is evident, but the broad streams of their posterity nevertheless are still distinguishable today.

The relationship and probable identification and geographic location of the sons of Noah and their descendants are indicated in the tables provided for quick reference. The discussion which follows each table provides further detail.

TABLE OF THE SONS OF JAPHETH
Genesis 10:2-5

Gomer — Ancient Cimmerians, the Gimirray of the Assyrians, Western Russia (Gen. 10:2, 3; I Chron. 1:5, 6; Ezek. 38:6).

Ashkenaz — Originally north of the Black Sea and the Caspian Sea (Gen. 10:3; I Chron. 1:6; Jer. 51:27). The name is evidently connected with cuneiform *Ashguza*, "Scythians."

Riphath — Location unknown, but probably included in modern Russia (Gen. 10:3; I Chron. 1:6).

Togarmah — Originally in Southwest Armenia, immigrating north and west (Gen. 10:3; I Chron. 1:6; cp. Ezek. 27:14; 38:6). This is Tegarama in cuneiform texts near Carchemish.

Magog — Probably the ancient Scythians, probably now in modern Russia (Gen. 10:2; I Chron. 1:5; Ezek. 38:2, 6; Rev. 20:8).

Madai — More commonly known as the Medes, originally south of the Caspian Sea (Gen. 10:2; I Chron. 1:5; cp. II Kings 17:6; 18:11; Ezra 6:2; Esth. 1:3, 14, 18, 19; Isa. 13:17; 21:2; Jer. 25:25; 51:11, 28; Dan. 5:28, 31; 6:8, 12, 15; 8:20; 9:1; 11:1; Acts 2:9).

Javan — Hellenists, Ionians, generally the Greek people, modern Greece (Gen. 10:2, 4; I Chron. 1:5, 7; Isa. 66:19; Ezek. 27: 13, 19; Dan. 8:21; 10:20; 11:2; Zech. 9:13).

Elishah — Inhabitants of Cyprus (Gen. 10:4; I Chron. 1:7; Ezek. 27:7). Corresponds to cuneiform *Alashiya,* Cyprus.

Tarshish — Location uncertain, but possibly inhabited Spain (from Tartessus in Spain) and Western Mediterranean (Gen. 10:4; I Chron. 1:7; cp. I Kings 10:22; 22:48; II Chron. 9:21; 20:36, 37; Pss. 48:7; 72:10; Isa. 2:16; 23:1, 6, 10, 14; 60:9; 66: 19; Jer. 10:9; Ezek. 27:12, 25; 38:13; Jonah 1:3; 4:2).

Kittim or Chittim — The Ionians, Greeks, and inhabited islands and coasts of Mediterranean Sea (Gen. 10:4; I Chron. 1:7; cp. Num. 24:24; Isa. 23:1, 12; Jer. 2:10; 25:22; 47:4; Ezek. 27:6; Dan. 11:30).

Dodanim — Lived in Illyricum and Troy, the entire region known as Dalmatia in modern times, i.e., Southeastern Europe (Gen. 10:4; I Chron. 1:7). Some prefer reading of Rodanim, hence Island of Rhodes.

Tubal — Identified with ancient Scythians originally in Eastern Asia Minor, and later probably immigrating further north to modern Russia (Gen. 10:2; I Chron. 1:5; Isa. 66:19; Ezek. 27:13; 32:26; 38:2, 3; 39:1).

Meshech — Originally in Eastern Asia Minor, later farther north in modern Russia (Gen. 10:2; I Chron. 1:5; Ezek. 27:13; 32:26; 38:2, 3; 39:1).

Tiras — Originally in Eastern Asia Minor, later in modern Russia (Gen. 10:2; I Chron. 1:5).

The sons of Japheth were more prolific in number than any of the other sons of Noah, and world history since the birth of Christ has largely featured those who were descendants of the seven sons of Japheth.

Japheth's son Gomer (Genesis 10:3) first mentioned in the list, according to Herodotus was the forefather of the Cimmerians. As a family in their early history, they conquered Urartu (Armenia) coming from their original Ukranian home where they lived before 800 B.C. They first appear in historical records as among the early enemies of Assyria and are mentioned prophetically in Ezekiel 38:6. There seems to be some evidence that they emigrated north ultimately out of Armenia into what today is known as Russia.

The three sons of Gomer are mentioned in Genesis 10:3 and also in I Chronicles 1:6, namely, Ashkenaz (cp. I Chronicles 1:6; Jeremiah 51:27), usually identified with the Scythians who lived north of the Black Sea and the Caspian Sea and spread over inner Asia. Others believe, however, that the Scythians are better identified as related to Magog. Riphath was another son of Gomer (cp. I Chronicles 1:6), but little is known about his descendants. Togarmah (cp. I Chronicles 1:6; Ezekiel 27:14; 38:6) appears occasionally in both history and prophecy. Descendants of Togarmah can be located in the fourteenth century B.C. as inhabiting Southwest Armenia. They are mentioned as furnishing horses, horsemen, and mules to Tyre (Ezekiel 27:14). Prophetically they are included in the invading host of Ezekiel 38:5, 6. Speaking generally, the descendants of Gomer inhabit the area north of the Holy Land and eventually emigrated north and east.

The second son of Japheth, Magog (cp. I Chronicles 1:5), is probably to be identified with the ancient Scythians (cp. discussion of Ashkenaz, above). Little mention is made of them historically except in these genealogies. Prophetically they are included in the invading horde of Ezekiel 38:2, 6 and again in Revelation 20:8. Speaking in general, they seem to have inhabited the area north of the Holy Land and could be one of the major elements in the population of Russia.

The third son of Japheth called Madai (cp. I Chronicles 1:5) is known more familiarly by the title given his descendants, the name *Medes,* who lived in Media south of the Caspian Sea bordered on the east by Hyrcania and Parthia, on the west by Assyria and Armenia and by Persia and Susiana on the south. The Medes are mentioned frequently in the Bible (II Kings 17:6; 18:11; Ezra 6:2; Esther 1:3, 14, 18, 19; Isaiah 13:17; 21:2; Jeremiah 25:25; 51:11, 28; Daniel 5:28, 31; 6:8, 12, 15; 8:20; 9:1; 11:1; Acts 2:9).

The Medes formed an important division of the times of the

Gentiles as prophesied by Daniel. They occupy a large share in the prophetic program of the Old Testament leading up to Christ. The height of the power of the Medes, after several centuries of struggle, was reached in the sixth century B.C. when the kingdom of the Medes was merged with that of Persia under Cyrus. Their notable triumph was the conquering of Babylon in 539 B.C. as recorded in Daniel 5. The Medes flourished for two centuries thereafter until the time of Alexander the Great.

The fourth son of Japheth known as Javan (cp. I Chronicles 1:5, 7) was the forefather of the Ionians or the Greeks. Descendants of Javan are mentioned in inscriptions of Assyria and Achaemenia. They were the Hellenists and the word *Javan* is so translated in the Septuagint. The descendants of Javan are mentioned frequently in the Bible (Isaiah 66:19; Ezekiel 27:13, 19; Daniel 8:21; 10:20; 11:2; Zechariah 9:13). The descendants of Javan inhabited Libya, and Caria, the Aegean Islands and the area known in modern history as Greece. As early as the eighth century B.C. Assyrian records mention a naval battle with the Greeks.

The four sons of Javan, Elishah, Tarshish, Kittim, and Dodanim do not appear as major elements in subsequent history. The descendants of Elishah seem to have inhabited Cyprus, referred to as the "isles of Elishah" (Ezekiel 27:7). They exported purple and scarlet fabrics to the market at Tyre, the purple dye being derived from shells rich in this color on the Aegean coasts.

The name *Tarshish* is found in the Phoenician language, meaning *smelting plant* and is closely associated with the smelting and transportation of smelted ores from distant places such as Spain in the Western Mediterranean and Solomon's copper smelting works in Southern Arabia. As ships were used to carry the smelted ore, frequent mention is made to ships of Tarshish (cp. I Kings 22:49, 50; II Chronicles 20:36, 37). Some believe the term also applies to any large ship regardless of geography (Psalm 48:7; Isaiah 23:1; 60:9; Ezekiel 27:25). It is therefore not clear whether the name *Tarshish* as the description of a descendant of Javan is the proper meaning in these many references and there may be no racial connection.

Kittim (sometimes spelled Chittim), another son of Javan, seems also to refer to the Ionian or Greeks. Although the name with various significations is found in a loose way to refer to the islands and coasts of the Mediterranean without specifying any particular geographic location, the name Kittim occurs with varied spellings elsewhere in the Old Testament (cp. Numbers 24:24; Isaiah 23:1, 12; Jeremiah 2:10; 25:22; 47:4; Ezekiel 27:6; Daniel 11:30). It is not clear to what extent Kittim is related to these references.

Dodanim (Genesis 10:4; I Chronicles 1:7), the fourth son of Javan, is regarded as the progenitor of those who lived in Illyricum and Troy and were closely associated with Kittim. They are relatively unimportant in subsequent Scriptures.

The three remaining sons of Japheth are named without posterity, signifying that their descendants did not form an important segment of the human race. Tubal (Genesis 10:2; I Chronicles 1:5) seems to be related to the Scythians. Their normal home seems to be near the Black Sea in Eastern Asia Minor. They are subsequently mentioned in the prophets (Isaiah 66:19; Ezekiel 27:13; 32:26; 38:2, 3; 39:1). Prophetically they will join with the invading army of the land of Israel in the last days recorded in Ezekiel 38 - 39. It is probable that their modern descendants now live in Russia.

Meshech appears in history as early as the twelfth century B.C. when his descendants lived to the north of Assyria in the Black Sea area. In Ezekiel 27:13, the descendants of Meshech had commercial dealings with Tyre, selling slaves and vessels of bronze. Prophetically, Meshech has a place in the last days as recorded in Ezekiel 32:26; 38:2,3; 39:1 and is included in the invading army.

Tiras the last son of Japheth is mentioned only in the genealogies (I Chronicles 1:5) and it is generally believed that his descendants became the Thracians who inhabited the Aegean coast.

The descendants of Japheth spread out to the north, east, and west, and are probably the progenitors of most of the Northern Europe lands and, hence, of all countries derived from Europe such as the United States and Canada. They formed the major part of the Gentiles or the nations and will have their important role in the chapters of world history which will bring the times of the Gentiles to conclusion.

TABLE OF THE SONS OF HAM
Genesis 10:6-20

In general the sons of Ham inhabited all of Asia except the north, and lived in Southern Europe and Northern Africa.

Cush — Southern Egypt, Abyssinia, Nubia, and Ethiopia (Gen. 10: 6-12).

Seba — Ancient Sabeans (Gen. 10:7; I Chron. 1:9; Ps. 72:10; Isa. 43:3; cp. "Sabeans," Job 1:15; Isa. 45:14; Ezek. 23:42; Joel 3:8; also "Sheba," I Kings 10; II Chron. 9; Job 6:19; Ps. 72:10, 15; Isa. 60:6; Jer. 6:20; Ezek. 27:22, 23; 38:13).

Havilah — Modern Yemen (Gen. 10:7; I Chron. 1:9; cp. Gen. 2:11; 10:29; 25:18; I Sam. 15:7; I Chron. 1:23).

Sabtah — Located East of Yemen (Gen. 10:7; I Chron. 1:9).

Raamah — His sons, Sheba and Dedan, and their descendants, inhabited Southwest Arabia (Gen. 10:7; I Chron. 1:9; Ezek. 27:22).

Sabtechah — Inhabited the eastern side of the Persian Gulf (Gen. 10:7; I Chron. 1:9).

Nimrod — Famous progenitor of inhabitants of Mesopotamia, Asshur, Nineveh, and Babylon. Also related to Erech, Accad, Calneh, Rehoboth, Calah, and Resen (Gen. 10:9-12; I Chron. 1:10; Micah 5:6). Some of these may be descriptive nouns rather than names of cities.

Mizraim — Egypt and East of Egypt (Gen. 10:13, 14; I Chron. 1: 11, 12; cp. all references to Egypt). All these names are plural emphasizing their ethnic character.

Ludim — Not yet identified but may be Libyans, North Africa (Gen. 10:13; I Chron. 1:11).

Anamim — Northern and Middle Egypt (Gen. 10:13; I Chron. 1:11).

Lehabim — Related to Libyans (Gen. 10:13; I Chron. 1:11).

Naphtuhim — Northern Egypt, Thebes, and Memphis (Gen. 10:13; I Chron. 1:11).

Pathrusim — Same location as Naphtuhim or may be Upper Egypt (Gen. 10:14; I Chron. 1:12).

Casluhim — Originally in Nile delta in Egypt, possibly inhabited Philistia later (Gen. 10:14; I Chron. 1:12). Some identify them as from Crete (cp. Deut. 2:23; Jer. 47:4; Amos 9:7).

Caphtorim — Origin same as Casluhim, possibly inhabited Philistia (Gen. 10:14; I Chron. 1:12).

Phut or Put — Generally Egypt, and Libya (Gen. 10:6; I Chron. 1:8; Isa. 66:19; Jer. 46:9; Ezek. 27:10; 30:5; 38:5; Nah. 3:9).

Canaan — At the time of the conquest all the land designated as

Palestine, west of the Jordan (Gen. 10:15-18; I Chron. 1:8, 13-16; etc., over 150 Old Testament references).

Sidon — Ancient Phoenicia, city of Sidon (Gen. 10:15; I Chron. 1:13; etc., about 40 Old Testament references and 12 New Testament references).

Heth — The ancient Hittites, a major civilization in Asia Minor (Gen. 10:15; I Chron. 1:13; etc., about 60 Old Testament references).

Jebusite — Original inhabitants of Jerusalem (Gen. 10:16; Josh. 15:63; Judg. 1:21; II Sam. 5:6, 8; 24:16, 18; I Chron. 1:14; 11:6; 21:18; Ezra 9:1; Neh. 9:8; Zech. 9:7; etc., about 35 Old Testament references).

Amorite — Located originally west of the Dead Sea (Gen. 10:16; I Chron. 1:14; etc., about 100 Old Testament references).

Girgashite — Located in Southern Palestine West of Jordan (Gen. 10:16; 15:21; Deut. 7:1; Josh. 3:10; 24:11; I Chron. 1:14; Neh. 9:8).

Hivite — Northern Palestine, Shechem (Gen. 10:17; I Chron. 1:15; etc., about 25 Old Testament references).

Arkite — North of Sidon (Gen. 10:17; I Chron. 1:15).

Sinite — North of Lebanon (Gen. 10:17; I Chron. 1:15).

Arvadite — Located on an island off the coast of Phoenicia, familiar in Assyrian records (Gen. 10:18; I Chron. 1:16; Ezek. 27:8, 11).

Zemarite — West of Galilee (Gen. 10:18; I Chron. 1:16; cp. Josh. 18:22; II Chron. 13:4).

Hamathite — Upper Syria, at the foot of Lebanon (Gen. 10:18; I Chron. 1:16; etc., over 35 Old Testament references).

The sons of Ham occupy a large portion of the Genesis 10 record (10:6-20; cp. I Chronicles 1:8-16). Four sons of Ham are mentioned in Genesis 10:6: Cush, Mizraim, Phut, and Canaan. Unquestionably the large space given to the sons of Ham was due to their ultimate relationship to the subsequent history of Israel and the purposes of God in the Middle East.

First mentioned of the sons of Ham is Cush whose descendants are enumerated as Seba, Havilah, Sabtah, Raamah, and Sabtechah. Special mention is made of the sons of Raamah, namely, Sheba and Dedan. The most prominent son of Cush, however, is Nimrod mentioned in Genesis 10:8-12.

In general the descendants of Ham occupy all of Asia except

the northern part, and settled in Southern Europe, and Northern Africa. They may be the forefathers of the American Indians who are believed to have originally entered the American continent through Alaska, having come up the east coast of Asia. The descendants of Cush seem to have inhabited Southern Egypt and the land to the south and east of Egypt, including ancient Abyssinia, Nubia, and Ethiopia. Because of the close proximity of the Semitic race, the Ethiopian language eventually became Semitic even though the racial origin was otherwise.

The five sons of Cush seem to refer to various peoples in the general geographic area of Egypt. Some of them reached all the way to the Persian Gulf and some mention is made of most of them in various Scriptures: Seba (cp. I Chronicles 1:9; Psalm 72: 10; Isaiah 43:3; cp. references to Sabeans, Job 1:15; Isaiah 45:14; Ezekiel 23:42; Joel 3:8; and references to Sheba, I Kings 10; II Chronicles 9; Job 6:19; Psalm 72:10, 15; Isaiah 60:6; Jeremiah 6: 20; Ezekiel 27:22, 23; 38:13). Havilah seems to refer to Southwestern Arabia known in modern times as Yemen (Genesis 10:7; I Chronicles 1:9; cp. Genesis 2:11; 10:29; 25:18; I Samuel 15:7; I Chronicles 1:23). Little is known of Sabtah except that probably it is to the east of Yemen (Genesis 10:7; I Chronicles 1:9). The descendants of Sabtah lived east of Yemen. The descendants of Raamah (Genesis 10:7; I Chronicles 1:9) are mentioned in Ezekiel 27:22 as famous traders and according to inscriptions were located geographically in Southwest Arabia adjacent to the Persian Gulf. Sabtechah (Genesis 10:7; I Chronicles 1:9) may have lived on the eastern side of the Persian Gulf.

The two sons of Raamah, namely, Sheba and Dedan are usually mentioned together and there is some confusion between Sheba and Seba (cp. Seba, above). Both lived in the general area of Arabia.

The special mention of Nimrod (Genesis 10:9-12; I Chronicles 1:10; cp. Micah 5:6) as a descendant of Cush is occasioned by the fact that he is the originator of Babel later known as Babylon and apparently was an energetic man who with his posterity built the Mesopotamian area and such famous spots as Asshur and Nineveh (Genesis 10:11). Nimrod was unquestionably the Napoleon of his day and the head of one of the earliest empires subsequent to Noah recorded in Scripture. His government seems to have occupied most of Western Asia and has left many monuments. The politi-

cal might symbolized in Nimrod and his empire was ended subsequent to the divine judgment at the tower of Babel when their
one language was confounded.

The second son of Ham, Mizraim, was the progenitor of the
major population of Egypt and usually the term is translated *Egypt*
(about 87 times) in its many instances in the Bible. It is generally
agreed, however, that the descendants of Mizraim, of which seven
are named (Genesis 10:13, 14), migrated to the east and this ac-
counts for the similarity between those who inhabited the area
adjacent to the Indian Ocean to the Egyptians. Ludim apparently
refers to the Libyans of Northern Africa. Anamim is mentioned
only in the genealogies (Genesis 10:13; I Chronicles 1:11) but
probably lived in Northern or Middle Egypt. Lehabim is also mentioned only in the genealogies (Genesis 10:13; I Chronicles 1:11)
and they also have been related to the Libyans. Naphtuhim and
Pathrusim (Genesis 10:13, 14; I Chronicles 1:12) seem to be related to Northern Egypt and especially the area around Thebes and
Memphis. Casluhim and Caphtorim (Genesis 10:14; I Chronicles
1:12) were in the Nile Delta area of Egypt. In general Mizraim is
therefore to be identified with Egypt, but its people migrated ex-
tensively to the east. As one of the important nations related to
Israel, they figure largely in subsequent prophecy and form one of
the great prophetic themes of the Old Testament which will be the
subject of later discussion.

The third son of Ham, Phut or Put, is mentioned a number of
times in the Bible (Genesis 10:6; I Chronicles 1:8; Isaiah 66:19;
Jeremiah 46:9; Ezekiel 27:10; 30:5; 38:5; Nahum 3:9). From these
references it is clear that the people who descended from Phut
were Africans closely associated with the descendants of Mizraim.
Their exact geographic location, however, is not clear and it may
be that they were scattered. Most probable identifications are that
they lived in Libya and other considerations have led some to think
that they lived south of Egypt or east of Egypt around the Red
Sea. Phut is mentioned in Isaiah 66:19 (spelled "Pul") along with
other nations to whom God will send a sign at the beginning of the
millennial kingdom. In Jeremiah 46:9 where the Hebrew *Put* is
translated "Libyans," they are the objects of God's judgment along
with Egypt. Mercenary soldiers from Phut were used by Tyre
(Ezekiel 27:10) and by Egypt (Jeremiah 46:9). They are again
associated with the fall of Egypt in Ezekiel 30:5 where they are

described as from "Libya." Prophetically they are included in the host which invade Israel in Ezekiel 38:5 where they are again described as coming from Libya. According to Nahum 3:9 their mercenary soldiers also helped Nineveh. The fact that the descendants of Phut are not described would indicate that they do not occupy a major role among the Gentiles.

The last son of Ham, Canaan, is obviously important to Biblical history and to the nation Israel. Eleven branches of descendants are mentioned in Genesis 10:15-18, "And Canaan begat Sidon his firstborn, and Heth, And the Jebusite, and the Amorite, and the Girgasite, And the Hivite, and the Arkite, and the Sinite, And the Arvadite, and the Zemarite, and the Hamathite."

The firstborn of Canaan, Sidon, is prominent in Scripture and descendants of Sidon probably formed the inhabitants of the ancient Phoenician city of Sidon or Zidon located some twenty miles north of Tyre. His descendants are first mentioned in the Amarna letters about 1400 B.C. and are prominent in Biblical history from the time of the conquest (Joshua 19:28). It became a city located in the territory of Asher and later was given the modern name of Saida. The city and its inhabitants are mentioned about forty times in the Old Testament and a dozen times in the New Testament. Its history is bound up with that of the Phoenicians from the eleventh and the eighth centuries B.C. and there is constant mention of them throughout the history of the Old Testament. On at least one occasion Christ preached in this area (Mark 7:24, 31) and condemned the sins of its inhabitants (Matthew 11:21-24). Paul also visited the city on his way to Rome (Acts 27:3). The prophets Isaiah, Jeremiah, and Ezekiel, all pronounced solemn judgments upon Sidon (Isaiah 23:2-12; Jeremiah 25:22; 27:3; 47:4; Ezekiel 27:8; 28:20-24; cp. Joel 3:4; Zechariah 9:2). Their prominence in Biblical history and prophecy is undoubtedly due to their geographic location and their close proximity to Tyre which was the special object of divine wrath.

Heth, the second son of Canaan, was the progenitor of the Hittites who figure prominently in Old Testament history. The Hittites are mentioned forty-seven times by this name in the Old Testament and fourteen times as the sons of Heth. Abraham's dealings with them are mentioned in Genesis 23 and the desire of Rebekah to avoid intermarriage with them is indicated in Genesis

27:46. The Hittites are included among the heathen nations with whom the Israelites had to deal in the conquest of the land. Even in David's time Uriah the Hittite is mentioned as the husband of Bathsheba, indicating the intermarriage of the Hittites with Israelites.

The center of the Hittite civilization, now uncovered by archaeologists, was in Asia Minor, and there is evidence that they had an important civilization and extensive literature and times of unusual political power especially during the period 1400-1200 B.C. Some have classified the Hittites as third in importance in the Middle East, with the Egyptians and the inhabitants of Mesopotamia surpassing them. The Hittites do not seem to be vitally connected with the prophetic program of Scripture.

The remaining descendants of Canaan each had their important influence on Biblical history. The Jebusites originally inhabited Jerusalem itself (Joshua 15:63) and their military might was indicated in the fact that the tribes were not able to dislodge them completely, and for many years they continued to live on the border between Judah and Benjamin (Joshua 15:63; Judges 1:21). They do not seem to have loomed large in the history of Israel although there is occasional mention throughout the Old Testament (cp. II Samuel 5:6, 8; 24:16, 18; I Chronicles 11:6; 21:18; Ezra 9:1; Nehemiah 9:8; Zechariah 9:7; and a number of other references).

The Amorites are prominent in Biblical history, being mentioned almost a hundred times in the Old Testament. They were one of the principal nations conquered by Israel in the conquest of the land and lived originally west of the Dead Sea. Their history is recorded, not only in the Scriptures, but in the inscriptions in which they were known as the Ammuru, with a history that extends from before Abraham. Their importance is mostly historical and they do not figure in prophecy except in predictions which were fulfilled in the conquest.

The Girgashites, living west of Jordan, also were one of the nations dispossessed by Israel in the time of the conquest. They are mentioned only seven times in the Old Testament (Genesis 10:16; 15:21; Deuteronomy 7:1; Joshua 3:10; 24:11; I Chronicles 1:14; Nehemiah 9:8). They have no role in the prophetic future.

The Hivites were also significant as a nation dispossessed by

Israel in the conquest. They seem to have lived in the northern part of the Holy Land, and they are mentioned about twenty-five times in the Old Testament usually in connection with other heathen countries whom Israel conquered. At one time they inhabited Shechem (Genesis 34).

The descendants of Canaan described as Arkites can be located some eighty miles north of Sidon and their name has been perpetuated in modern times by the city Tell Arka. This locality had a long history recorded outside the Bible as early as 1400 B.C., but is mentioned in the Bible only in Genesis 10:7 and I Chronicles 1:15 in the genealogies.

The Sinites are referred to only in Genesis 10:17 and I Chronicles 1:15. No definite identification is possible, but it is probable that they are located in the northern part of Lebanon where Strabo refers to "Sinna" as a fort in the mountains. Several other obscure references are found to it in ancient literature.

The Arvadites, mentioned only four times in Scripture (Genesis 10:18; I Chronicles 1:16; Ezekiel 27:8-11), were inhabitants of the island Arvad located two miles from the shore off the coast of Phoenicia. Its modern name is Ruwad.

The Zemarites are cited in Genesis 10:18 and I Chronicles 1:16 and lived in the area west of Galilee between Arvad and Hamath. Other locations have been mentioned, such as Emessa, modern Hums, with others finding them at Sumra, or in the area of Mount Zemaraim (cp. Joshua 18:22; II Chronicles 13:4).

The Hamathites inhabited the city-state of Hamath in upper Syria, referred to about thirty-five times in the Old Testament. At one time an important Canaanite colony (Genesis 10:18), it was captured by the Assyrians in the time of Hezekiah (II Kings 18:34). Located at the foot of Lebanon, it had a long history and came under the control of Assyria, then a province of Syria, and eventually came under the government of Persia in Nehemiah's time. Undoubtedly the descendants of Canaan spread over considerable territory — from Sidon to Gaza and eastward as far as the area east of the Dead Sea as indicated in the mention of Sodom, Gomorrah, Admah, Zeboim, and Lasha in Genesis 10:19.

Taken as a whole, the sons of Ham lived in an extensive geographic area and were the original inhabitants of the land given by God to Israel.

TABLE OF THE SONS OF SHEM
Genesis 10:21-31

Elam — Eastern neighbor and traditional rival of Mesopotamian states, settled in a portion of Persia (Gen. 10:22; I Chron. 1:17; cp. Gen. 14:1, 9; Isa. 11:11; 21:2, 6; Jer. 25:25; 49: 34-39; Ezek. 32:24; Dan. 8:2).

Asshur — To be identified with Assyria (Gen. 10:22; I Chron. 1:17; cp. Num. 24:22, 24; Ezra 4:2; Ps. 83:8; Ezek. 27:23; 32:22; Hos. 14:3; and about 140 Old Testament references to Assyria).

Arphaxad — Located originally north and east of Nineveh (Gen. 10:22, 24, 25; 11:11-27; I Chron. 1:17-24; cp. Luke 3:36).

  Salah — Also spelled Shelah (Gen. 10:24; 11:12-15; I Chron. 1:18; Luke 3:35).

    Eber — Father of Hebrew race (Gen. 10:21, 24, 25; 11:14-17; I Chron. 1:18, 19, 25).

      Peleg — Progenitor of Abraham (Gen. 10:25; 11:16-19; I Chron. 1:19, 25).

      Joktan — His thirteen sons were progenitors of the Arabs (Gen. 10:25, 26, 29; I Chron. 1:19, 20, 23).

Lud — Associated with both Asiatic and African people, possible reference to Lydians of Anatolia, location uncertain (Gen. 10:22; I Chron. 1:17; Isa. 66:19; Ezek. 27:10).

Aram — Inhabited wide area in Syria and Mesopotamia (Gen. 10:22, 23; I Chron. 1:17; cp. also about 65 Old Testament references to Syrians, another name for descendants of Aram).

  Uz — Occupied Arabian desert west of Babylon (Gen. 10:23; I Chron. 1:17; cp. Job 1:1; Jer. 25:20; Lam. 4:21).

  Hul — Probably located near Lake Merom, north of Sea of Galilee (Gen. 10:23; I Chron. 1:17).

  Gether — Location unknown (Gen. 10:23; I Chron. 1:17).

  Mash — Also known as Meshech, location unknown (Gen. 10:23; I Chron. 1:17).

The third major division of the children of Noah were descendants of Shem, mentioned in Genesis 10:21-31. These were also known as "all the children of Eber" (Genesis 10:21). By this is meant that the children of Eber, who were descendants of Shem through Arphaxad and Salah, were descendants of Shem, but the term is not properly applied to all of the descendants of Shem. They were the more important descendants of Shem. It was from this line that Abraham and the children of Israel came (cp. Genesis 11:10-27).

Five sons of Shem are mentioned in Genesis 10:22. The descendants of Elam (Genesis 10:22; I Chronicles 1:17), seemed to have settled in that portion of Persia which bears their name (cp. Genesis 14:1, 9; Isaiah 11:11; 21:2, 6; Jeremiah 25:25; 49:34-39; Ezekiel 32:24; Daniel 8:2).

Asshur is mentioned second (Genesis 10:22; I Chronicles 1:17; cp. Numbers 24:22, 24; Ezra 4:2; Psalm 83:8; Ezekiel 27:23; 32:22; Hosea 14:3; and about 140 Old Testament references to Assyria). The descendants of Asshur lived in Assyria. They were the forerunners of the later mighty Assyrian Empire, having come originally from Babylon and having a close connection with the Babylonians throughout their subsequent history. As Assyria held a prominent place in the history of the ancient world from the ninth to the seventh century B.C., they had an important place in prophecy which has already been fulfilled.

Arphaxad (Genesis 10:22, 24, 25; 11:11-27; I Chronicles 1:17-24; cp. Luke 3:36) is important as progenitor of the line which led to Abraham and to Christ in the genealogies introduced in Genesis 10:24, 25 and amplified in Genesis 11:13-27. One of the important descendants of Arphaxad was Eber (Genesis 10:21, 24, 25; 11:14-17; I Chronicles 1:18, 19, 25), son of Salah, or Shelah (Genesis 11:12-15; I Chronicles 1:18, 24), who had two prominent sons, Peleg and Joktan. From Peleg (Genesis 10:25; 11:16-19; I Chronicles 1:19, 25) descended the line to Abraham. Joktan (Genesis 10:25, 26, 29; I Chronicles 1:19, 20, 23) had thirteen sons (Genesis 10:26-29). Almodad was the founder of one of the Arab tribes. Sheleph had descendants who probably settled in Sulaf. Hazarmaveth settled in a portion of Arabia; Jerah was another Arabian tribe. Hadoram was another Arabian tribe impossible to identify. Uzal is often connected with Sanaa, a city in Yemen. Diklah was the progenitor of a people who settled in Yemen; Obal fathered another Arabian tribe called Ebal in I Chronicles 1:22, whose location is unknown. The founder of an Arab tribe known as Mael was Abimael. Sheba was the forerunner of an important kingdom in Southern Arabia known as the kingdom of Sheba. Nothing seems to be known about Ophir. Havilah probably populated a portion of Southern Arabia. Jobab is the name of another Arabian tribe concerning whom little is known. The descendants of Joktan according to Genesis 10:30 lived in the area from Mesha unto Sephar, the area to the west and south of Babylon corresponding with Arabia Petraea.

Lud, the fourth son of Shem (Genesis 10:22; I Chronicles 1:17; Isaiah 66:19; Ezekiel 27:10), seems to have become associated with Ludim, descendants of Mizraim. Both Lud and Ludim are associated with peoples of Africa and Asia, but their precise location is not clear. One explanation is that the term may have referred to mercenary soldiers who because of the character of their work were scattered. They were employed by Egypt.

Aram (Genesis 10:22, 23; I Chronicles 1:17), the last named of the children of Shem, was the progenitor of a large offspring which inhabited a wide area of Syria and Mesopotamia. The word *Aram* is translated *Syrian* more than 65 times in the Old Testament. Uz (Genesis 10:23; I Chronicles 1:17; cp. Job 1:1; Jeremiah 25:20; Lamentations 4:21), a son of Aram, seems to have settled in Arabia west of Babylon, the scene of the Book of Job. Hul (Genesis 10:23; I Chronicles 1:17) and his descendants probably lived near Lake Merom on the Jordan north of Galilee. The location of Gether and Mash (Genesis 10:23; I Chronicles 1:17), who is also known as Meshech in I Chronicles 1:17, is unknown.

Important to the history of Israel is the fact that the wives of Jacob were Aramaic or Syrian (Deuteronomy 26:5). By the time of King Saul the Aramaeans had occupied several districts adjacent to Israel including the land between the Tigris and Euphrates; Damascus (I Kings 11:23, 24); Zobah (II Samuel 8), north of Hamath; Maachah (Joshua 12:5; 13:11), east of Jordan near Mount Hermon; Geshur (Deuteronomy 3:14; II Samuel 15:8; 13:37), east of the Sea of Galilee; Beth-Rehob (cp. Numbers 13:21; Judges 18:28), near Geshur; and Ish-tob (II Samuel 10:6), also east of Jordan.

From a Biblical standpoint, the descendants of Shem were most important because through them is traced the line of the Messiah, Abraham, and Israel. It is probably for this reason that they are mentioned last in the genealogy in contrast to the fact that they are mentioned first in Genesis 10:1.

The genealogies of the nations provide a framework of Biblical prophecy. While many of the nations do not figure largely or prominently, the outworking of the divine purpose inevitably stems from these early progenitors of the human race. The fact that they are itemized in Scripture indicates that from the divine viewpoint these constitute the outline of the divine purpose in human history.

CHAPTER III

ISRAEL AND THE NATIONS

The selection of Abraham as the progenitor of a new division of humanity was a dramatic milestone in the history of mankind. It may be compared to the creation of Adam and Eve following the prehistoric fall of some of the holy angels led by Satan, and was similar to the new beginning with Noah after the destruction of the rest of humanity by the flood. The sovereign choice of Abraham marked a new and significant development in the progressive unfolding of God's purpose in the world.

The fact that Genesis itself devotes only eleven chapters to the whole history of the universe up to Abraham and then uses the remainder of almost forty chapters to trace the life of Abraham, Isaac, and Jacob, in itself demonstrates the tremendous significance of this new development. From Genesis 11:10, where the genealogy of Abraham is given, to the last book of the Bible, Revelation, the seed of Abraham is constantly in the foreground, and the Gentiles are introduced only as they are related to the history of Israel. No approach to a proper understanding of Scripture can ignore this obvious divine emphasis upon the numerically small people who descended from Jacob. The explanation is not in any peculiarity of the people of Israel, but rather in the sovereign choice of God in selecting them to fulfill His purpose. Three major areas tell the story of the relation of Israel to the nations.

THE DIVINE PURPOSE IN REDEMPTION

Unquestionably one of the principal reasons for the selection of Abraham and his posterity was the divine purpose to fulfill the promise given to Adam and Eve that the seed of the woman would bruise the head of the serpent (Genesis 3:15). The divine intention to fulfill this through Abraham's posterity is embodied in the promise, "in thee shall all families of the earth be blessed" (Genesis 12:3). The primary importance of Israel rests in the fact that

41

through them God would fulfill His purpose to reveal His grace and provide redemption in Christ. Through this provision not only would God redeem the nation of Israel, but also those in all of the nations who would turn to God and Christ in faith. The spiritual seed of Abraham according to Galatians 3:7 are all those who like Abraham trust in God.

No philosophy of history is complete unless it includes recognition of God's redemptive plan from the standpoint of eternity. The important factor in every life as well as in every nation is the fulfillment of God's redemptive purpose to save those by grace who believe. Life becomes meaningless except as it is related to Jesus Christ as Saviour and Lord and as it is related to eternity by receiving eternal life in time. If it were not for God's redemptive purpose, life as well as history would be a hopeless puzzle without motivation and objective, and God and His purposes would be an unsolvable enigma.

THE DIVINE PURPOSE IN REVELATION

Important as is the divine purpose in salvation, however, this is only one aspect, although a major aspect, to be found in God's selection of Abraham and his posterity. If the major reason for God creating the universe and man is to use the world as a means of declaring His own ineffable glory, then the selection of Abraham also assumes major importance because through Abraham's seed God purposed to reveal Himself. This revelation came first through prophets, such as Abraham himself, through whom God spoke. Most important were the writers of Scripture such as Moses and those who succeeded him. Most if not all of the Bible was written by those who were physical descendants of Abraham. It was through Abraham that not only Christ came, 'but also the prophets. Although God on occasion spoke through Gentiles, as in the dreams of Nebuchadnezzar, these were incidental rather than central in God's usual method of revealing Himself through history.

The final and climactic revelation was of course in the person of Jesus Christ who in the incarnation not only became man, but revealed God through human flesh. Christ was not only the way of salvation, but He was also the way of revelation. All of this was included in the purpose of God in divine revelation in selecting Abraham and his descendants. The choice of Abraham as the channel through which both redemption and divine revelation should come introduces another important factor often overlooked in the theological analysis of God's promises to Abraham and their fulfillment.

THE DIVINE PURPOSE IN THE HISTORY OF ISRAEL

God was not only going to use Israel as a means of redemption and a means of revelation, but their very history and prophecy were to be a cameo which would reveal God in His dealings with mankind in general. The history of Israel in the Old Testament in their relationship to the Gentiles is also a spiritual analysis of human experience as the people of God seek to live in a temporal world. The careful recital of Israel's failures and successes and the principles which guided their rise or fall according to Romans 15:4 "were written aforetime . . . for our learning, that we through patience and comfort of the scriptures might have hope."

The relationship of Israel to the nations therefore forms not only an important background for understanding "the times of the Gentiles" (Luke 21:24) and God's dealings with nations other than Israel, but also makes clear the role of the Gentiles in God's purpose in history. It was to be in the context of their relationship to the nations that Israel was to reveal their particular qualities as a people of God. In this they illustrated the timeless spiritual principles that are involved in a people of God living in a world which is basically anti-God. The history of Israel in relation to the nations prior to the times of the Gentiles and the Babylonian captivity may be divided into seven subdivisions.

Israel in Egypt. Abraham, Isaac, and Jacob, although promised the land as a perpetual possession of their seed, never actually possessed the Promised Land. Instead, as God predicted in Genesis 15:13, 14, "Know of a surety that thy seed shall be a stranger in a land that is not theirs, and shall serve them; and they shall afflict them four hundred years; And also that nation, whom they shall serve, will I judge; and afterward shall they come out with great substance." This prophecy of Israel's relationship to Egypt was fulfilled in Genesis 46 when Jacob and his family followed Joseph to the land of Egypt to avoid the famine in the Promised Land.

The sojourn of the children of Israel in Egypt for 430 years (1876-1446 B.C.) increased the people of Israel from 70 to approximately 3,000,000. Their rapid increase in numbers and wealth aroused the opposition of the Egyptian kings. Israel soon became an enslaved people first under the Hyksos rulers who displaced the native Egyptian kings in the period 1730-1580 B.C., and later when the Egyptian kings were able to resume control at which time the iniquitous law requiring the killing of all male children in Israel was imposed. During the reign of Amenhotep II (1447-1421 B.C.), after the imposition of the ten plagues upon Egypt, the nation of Israel was finally expelled from Egypt and the Exodus began. This probably occurred in 1446 B.C., although some critical scholars favor a date as late as 1290 B.C. During the years of their growth in Egypt, God had marvelously begun the preparation of the Promised Land for their occupation. Now, however, it was necessary to temper and discipline the nation Israel for their new role as a separate people inheriting the promises of God.

Israel in the wilderness wanderings. During the forty years in which Israel wandered in the wilderness, they were the objects of God's special care in a way that no people had ever previously experienced. The Exodus from Egypt had been preceded by the miraculous intervention of God in the plagues inflicted upon the Egyptians. This had been supported by the great deliverance from the hosts of the Egyptians at the Red Sea when a miraculous strong wind permitted the Israelites to cross the sea as on dry land, but the Egyptians were engulfed by the returning waters when they attempted to follow.

In the first year of their wilderness wanderings at Mount Sinai, Israel was introduced to the covenant of the law which involved for them not only the obligation to keep a particular rule of life, but to be "a kingdom of priests, and an holy nation" (Exodus 19: 6). The comprehensive revelation given to Moses of Israel's moral, ceremonial, and social law as well as the order of worship and the details of the construction of the Tabernacle and its furniture was a tremendous disclosure of God which was greeted almost immediately by rebellion on the part of the people as recorded in Exodus 32.

It was subsequent to this preliminary failure that Israel, after sending out spies to survey the land for forty days, accepted the unfavorable report of the ten spies that the land could not be conquered. Because of their spiritual immaturity and lack of faith, Israel rebelled against God and was saved from extermination only by Moses' intercession (Numbers 14). The subsequent disciplinary judgment of God declared that all the adults would die in the wilderness during forty years of wandering, whereas their little ones whom they said would fall prey to the enemy would inherit the promise of possession of the land (Numbers 14:28-34).

During the wilderness wanderings, for the most part, Israel did not engage in fighting with existing tribes, but their few contacts with other nations were unhappy chapters in the years of their wandering. In Numbers 20:21 Edom, the descendants of Esau, Jacob's twin brother, refused to let Israel pass through their territory. This began a history of long enmity between Israel and Edom which will continue throughout the times of the Gentiles.

Another traditional enemy of Israel was Sihon of Heshbon, an Amorite, and a descendant of one of the eleven sons of Canaan who also opposed the children of Israel. His opposition, however, was used of God to destroy him as the children of Israel took all of his cities and destroyed them utterly from Aroer to Gilead, that is, most of the land east of Jordan from Galilee to the Dead Sea. Their subsequent contacts with Og King of Bashan, another division of the Amorites, resulted in a similar disaster for Og and his people. They too were exterminated, and the children of Israel occupied this territory, the land to the east of Galilee and somewhat to the north. These preliminary victories at the close of the years of wandering were the forerunner of the conquering of the land west of Jordan. Also illustrated is the spiritual conflict be·tween a people of God and those who are anti-God as represented in their enemies.

The conquering of the Promised Land. With the death of Moses, Joshua succeeded him as the leader of Israel, and the book that bears his name records the subsequent conquest of the land. Most of the territory west of Jordan was nominally under the control of Egypt whose King Amenhotep III reigned from approximately 1412-1376 B.C. He had neglected Palestine to the point that its political government was largely conducted by city-states over which there was only lax supervision. They were accordingly ill-prepared to resist an aggressive, co-ordinated attack from the nation Israel.

Israel crossed the Jordan through a miraculous stopping of the waters during the flood state probably in the spring of 1406 B.C. Their conquest of Jericho was aided by a supernatural destruction of the walls subsequently. After an initial defeat, in a second attack they conquered Ai with the result that the larger city Bethel (Joshua 8) was likewise conquered. The southern portion of the land west of Jordan was possessed first by Gibeon who through trickery secured a treaty and then by the defeat of the alliance of five Amorite kings who had besieged Gibeon (10:1-27). Their victory was aided by the supernatural long day of Joshua 10:12-14. The conquest of other kings including Jabin, King of Hazor (Joshua 11:1-11) resulted in the bulk of the land falling to Israel during the first six years of the conquest. Joshua, now approaching old age, arranged for the division of the land even though many of the Canaanites still retained potential for opposition, and some of the land had not yet been possessed. The victory, although tremendous and allowing living space for Israel, was far short of what God had promised if they would truly possess the land by faith (Joshua 1:2-5). They failed to carry out the command of Moses to exterminate completely the Canaanites. The utter immorality and false religions of the Canaanites were to prove so damaging to the people of Israel that it led to the extended period of political anarchy and moral decay which characterized the period of the judges.

The period of the Judges. The early verses of Judges record some of the preliminary victories against the Canaanites. But even before the end of the first chapter the sad record is given: "The children of Benjamin did not drive out the Jebusites that inhabited Jerusalem" (Judges 1:21). Nor did the children of Manasseh conquer the Canaanites that dwelt in their area, but rather put them under tribute (1:27, 28). Similar failure of other tribes is recorded in verses 29-36. This disobedience of the express command of Moses (Deuteronomy 7:2) set up the situation for Israel's spiritual and political decay.

For more than three centuries Israel was ruled by judges often local in their influence and sometimes contemporary. The lesson repeatedly given, however, was that when Israel sinned, God would use the Gentiles to inflict disciplinary punishment and over-lordship upon them. When they genuinely repented, God would raise up a judge or leader to deliver them from their enemies. Their subsequent deliverance, however, was often short-lived, and they drifted back into the old sins. The book of Joshua is a spiral, but a spiral downward, and Israel's moral situation at the close of Judges was one of total anarchy ethically, religiously, and politically. Israel never sank lower than in the closing chapters of Judges. Such is the clear lesson of what happens to a nation with initial spiritual power when it joins socially and religiously as well as politically with the world totally debased and devoid of moral purity.

As in the later history of Israel, God used the Gentiles to inflict punishment upon the children of Israel. Among the more important enemies of Israel were the Hittites who lay to their north and the Egyptians who were to the south. Also prominent in the period were the Moabites, descendants of Lot, and Amalek, descendants of Esau (Judges 3:12-14). The Canaanites led by Jabin (Judges 4:1-3) were another who oppressed Israel.

In the time of Gideon, the Midianites were the instrument of oppression. Although their origin is obscure, they probably were descendants of Midian a son of Abraham by Keturah (Genesis 25: 1-6) who had inhabited much of the land east of Jordan and the Dead Sea. In the time of Moses they had accumulated considerable wealth as nomads (Numbers 31:22, 32-34). They did not figure largely in history outside the Bible and have long since disappeared. The remarkable deliverance by Gideon's three hundred is one of the bright chapters of Judges.

Among the other oppressors of Israel were the Philistines, an ancient people who inhabited the coastal region along the Mediterranean west of the Dead Sea. The Philistines had a long history, having apparently invaded the Middle East from the sea and engaged Raamses III (1195-1164 B.C.), ruler of Egypt, in a series of battles. The Philistines who survived settled in southeast Palestine and eventually gave the entire area the name Palestine, the Greek form of Philistia. The name Philistine appears in the Bible over two hundred times and in more than seventy different chapters.

In many respects the relationship of Israel to the Philistines was their spiritual barometer. When Israel was in the dominant position, it was a token of God's blessing. When they were in oppression by the Philistines, it was a sign of spiritual declension. Much of the closing material of Judges relates to the Philistines. It was not until the time of Samuel that Israel was rescued from forty years of domination by the Philistines (Judges 13:1).

Samuel and Eli the priest were the last two of the fourteen judges which prefaced the appointment of Saul as King. It was through Samuel that the crushing defeat of Israel at Ebenezer (I

Samuel 4), in which Eli and his sons died, was turned into a victory in a later battle recorded in I Samuel 7. Another attempt was made by the Philistines to gain power in the battle which resulted in the death of Saul and Jonathan (I Samuel 31). The period of the Judges was completely indecisive as far as victory for Israel is concerned, but is a record of human failure, contrasted to divine grace extended to a people when repentant. God's forgiveness was a demonstration of the faithfulness of God to a people who deserved judgment rather than mercy. The sovereign purpose of God in the nation Israel, though obscure in Judges, emerges more clearly in the period of the kingdoms.

The kingdoms of Saul, David, and Solomon. When Israel rejected the theocratic rule of God through judges and demanded that a king be appointed, God made clear that they were inviting oppressive rulers who would make slaves of their children and who would demand a large portion of their income. Their desire to be like the Gentiles was obviously born of the flesh rather than of the Spirit. In granting their request, however, prophecy was being fulfilled, for God had said to Abraham, "Kings shall come out of thee" (Genesis 17:6).

The first king to be appointed was Saul, anointed privately by Samuel, then later named publicly and finally confirmed after the victory at Jabesh-Gilead (I Samuel 11). Saul proved, however, to be an inept ruler, foolishly proud of his sovereignty and position, and jealous of David who had become a national hero by conquering Goliath. The fulfillment of the prophecy of his death in battle is recorded in the closing chapter of I Samuel and the first chapter of II Samuel. David immediately was proclaimed king over his own tribe of Judah (II Samuel 2:4). After a period of civil war and the death of Ish-bosheth the ruler of the ten tribes, he became king over all Israel about 1003 B.C. Among the first achievements of his reign was the complete rout of the Philistines.

The reign of David occurred at a time in which neighboring nations were in a weakened or inefficient state and unable to counter his rising power. The Hittites to the north had been broken by Barbarian invasions and rendered ineffective. Assyria likewise was in a weakened state, and Egypt was in a battle of power between the priests and merchants who alternately ruled from 1100 B.C. on. The reign of David was a glorious achievement of a man whom God had blessed and who was gifted as a warrior, general, and king. His power extended from the Euphrates River to the northeast, to the Mediterranean to the west, and the Red Sea to the south.

His long reign was not without its complications. His lax discipline of his sons, the product of multiple marriages, his crime in relation to Uriah and Bathsheba, and his sin in numbering the people were blots on his record. God nevertheless assured to him that his son would have a glorious reign, and in due time Solomon succeeded David.

In contrast to the experience of his father, Solomon's reign was one of peace and luxury, and social and cultural advance. He exceeded his father in multiple marriages, many of them with heathen women, with the result that his children were not brought up in the knowledge of the Lord (cp. Deuteronomy 17:17). He likewise violated the law in his reliance upon many chariots and military strength, instead of depending upon God (Deuteronomy 17:16). His luxurious living and demand for many buildings resulted in increased oppression and taxation which in turn led to the divided kingdom after his death.

The period of Saul, David, and Solomon was, from an outward standpoint, undoubtedly one of the most glorious in the history of Israel. Its outer glory, however, did not hide many spiritual failures which ultimately resulted in the captivities and the destruction of the monuments erected by David and Solomon.

The divided kingdoms of Judah and Israel. After the death of Solomon in 930 B.C. his son Rehoboam, who succeeded him, foolishly continued the oppressive taxation with the result that the ten tribes withdrew and formed the northern kingdom of Israel. Although endowed with many advantages over the kingdom of Judah, the kingdom of Israel from the start was a record of spiritual failure. Their reliance upon idols, commercial prosperity, and the fertility of the soil in their area led them to depart from God and to neglect the sanctuary in Jerusalem. The golden calves introduced by Jeroboam, their first king at Dan and Bethel, were blasphemous substitutes for the true worship of God.

The kings of Israel without exception were ungodly men, and the course of Israel was downward for the next two centuries ending in the captivity of the ten tribes by Assyria 721 B.C. The period was marked with warfare between Israel and Judah and at times both kingdoms were dominated by outsiders such as the Syrian domination 841-790 B.C. Although there were periods of prosperity and strength, as under Jeroboam II, when outside oppression was at a minimum, the path of the kingdom of Israel was downward.

The nation of Judah, composed of the two tribes Judah and Benjamin in and around Jerusalem, had the advantage of the spiritual strength of being the religious center of the nation. Although some of its kings were wicked men, there were periods of revival as under Hezekiah and Josiah. They only temporarily, however, and somewhat superficially brought the children of Israel back to God. Ultimately the two remaining tribes fell to the invading Medes and Babylonians, as prophesied by Nahum (3:18, 19). The Babylonian defeat of the Egyptians at Carchemish in 605 B.C. introduced the period of Babylonian domination which continued for more than a half century and made possible the captivity of the two remaining tribes, many of whom were carried off into ancient Babylon. The kings who would fight their enemies, which Israel had demanded of God, had brought only temporary prosperity. Morally, the period of the kings, especially the kings of Israel, was no better than the period of the judges. Israel had yet to learn the lessons that under the law blessing could be secured only by obedience. Although God was a gracious God who welcomed a repentant people, there was a high price to pay for neglect of the law and for worship of idols.

Post-captivity. In the captivity of Israel by Assyria and the captivity of Judah by the Babylonians, most of the population were carried off into captivity. The ten tribes suffered a series of deportations beginning in the reign of Pekah, king of Israel, when Tiglath-pileser III about 740 B.C. carried off the tribes to the east of Jordan to Assyria (I Chronicles 5:26) and some of those in Galilee (II Kings 15:29). In 721 B.C. Samaria was captured and more than 25,000 of the population went into captivity. Before the Babylonian captivity even began, it is estimated that 200,000 captives were taken from the ten tribes as well as the cities of Judah.

The Babylonian captivity began with the fall of Jerusalem 606 B.C. when selected captives including Daniel were carried off to Babylon. This was followed by a major deportation in 597 B.C. when 10,000 of the leaders of Judah were deported. Another major deportation took place in 586 B.C. when Jerusalem itself was destroyed.

The captivities continued until 538 B.C. when Cyrus issued a decree for a return of some of the pilgrims to their ancient land (Ezra 1:2). With the time taken to organize the expedition and return to their ancient land, the predicted seventy years was consumed between 606 B.C. and 536 B.C. in fulfillment of the prediction of seventy years of captivity (Jeremiah 25:11, 12; 29:10). The returning pilgrims, after some delay, were able to build the temple, completed about 516 B.C. or exactly seventy years after Jerusalem itself was laid desolate and the previous temple destroyed (Daniel 9:2).

The number of the returning pilgrims in the first expedition were 42,360 (Ezra 2:64). Their servants brought the total number to approximately 50,000. Most of these were from the tribes of Judah and Benjamin and Levi, but included some from other tribes. Some of those carried off in the Assyrian captivities returned as they were able, until all twelve tribes were represented. A later expedition led by Ezra (Ezra 7-10) further swelled the number of returning pilgrims. Under the leadership of Nehemiah the walls of the city were rebuilt and a plan for the rebuilding of the city itself was adopted and put into effect.

As the Old Testament closes, the children of Israel are back in the land, but always under some form of Gentile supervision and authority. The remaining centuries which led up to Christ were unhappy ones for Israel especially under the fearful persecutions of the Romans who according to Josephus slaughtered more than 1,000,000 Israelites in the siege of Jerusalem alone in A.D. 70. In the second century following Christ, Palestine was almost devoid of Jews, who had been scattered to the four winds. It was not until the twentieth century that Israel was restored to their ancient land and re-established as a nation there.

In the history of God's dealings with Israel He revealed His attributes in a way in which He did not reveal them to the Gentile world. To Israel, God had made many wonderful and everlasting promises. They were to be a people who would continue forever (Jeremiah 31:35-37). They were to have a king forever of the line of David (II Samuel 7:16). They were to have title to the land forever (Genesis 17:8).

These promises, though unfulfilled to generations which neglected the Word of God and trusted in idols made with hands, nevertheless manifest God's faithfulness in dealing with an erring people. Even in the midst of their apostasy and sin, when the prophets of God thundered warnings of divine judgment, there is the recurring note of God's unfailing purpose, of God's faithfulness to Abraham, Isaac, and Jacob. The certainty of the ultimate fulfillment of the promises is made clear as they are repeated again and again in the Old Testament Scriptures.

The relationship of the Gentiles to Israel is always that of a supporting role. God's sovereignty and divine power are again and again manifested in His dealings with the nations, but this is always subordinated to His purpose for Israel and the fulfillment of the spiritual promises to all who would trust in the God of Israel. The eternal shines again and again through the temporal, and the immediate actors on the stage are never allowed to forget that behind the scenes God is still directing the panorama of history to His desired and prophesied end. Prophecy concerning the Gentiles, accordingly, although more expansive in its character and worldwide in its significance, is always presented in Scripture in relation to God's purposes for Israel. World history which is not related to this is usually omitted in Scripture. The Biblical point of view, therefore, is quite different from that of the world in general to whom Israel was an insignificant people. From the standpoint of God's divine election, Israel is instead the key, and through Israel God was to fulfill His purpose whether redemptive, political, or eschatological.

Chapter IV

WORLD HISTORY IN OUTLINE

The study of Daniel is an indispensable introduction to the Biblical foreview of world history. Through Daniel came the revelation of the major events which would mark the progress of what Christ referred to as "the times of the Gentiles" (Luke 21:24). Christ defined this as the period during which "Jerusalem shall be trodden down of the Gentiles," i.e., from Nebuchadnezzar 606 B.C. until the second advent of Jesus Christ.

No system of philosophy or theology which attempts to arrive at the meaning of history can ignore this divine analysis of the progress of human events. The broad prophetic program for the nations when viewed alongside the prophetic program for Israel and the program of God in the present age for the church answers the major question of the divine purposes of God in history in which God reveals His glory.

In God's program for Israel, He has revealed His faithfulness, His love, and His righteousness. In His program for the church, the grace of God is supremely revealed. In the program of world history as a whole, God's dealings with the nations reveal His sovereignty, power, and wisdom. The nations may foolishly rage against God (Psalm 2:1), but God nevertheless shall triumphantly place His Son as King in Zion (Psalm 2:6).

DANIEL THE PROPHET

Daniel the prophet was born in the ill-fated days just preceding the captivity. As a lad he was apparently separated from his parents and carried captive to far away Babylon. There, because of his unusual intelligence and promise, he was trained along with his companions for service in the court of the king. It was only after Daniel had successfully completed this course of training and had demonstrated his wisdom and understanding (Daniel 1:20) that he faced the supreme test recorded in Daniel 2.

NEBUCHADNEZZAR'S DREAM

Nebuchadnezzar, the king of Babylon, had had a rapid rise to power, heading what is known in secular history as the Neo-Chaldean Empire. His father Nabopolassar had founded the empire in 625 B.C. His son Nebuchadnezzar had won an outstanding victory over Necho of Egypt at Carchemish in 605 B.C. and in the process of his conquest had conquered and later destroyed Jerusalem, carrying off many of the Jews as captives. According to Daniel 2:29, the king had pondered the practical question of "what should come to pass hereafter." What would be the end result of his great victories and magnificent kingdom? It was in such a state of mind that God gave to Nebuchadnezzar a prophetic dream.

Aware of the fact that the dream had tremendous significance, but unable to recall its details, he called in his wise men and demanded that they show him the dream and its interpretation. Brushing aside their protest that this was an unreasonable request, when they were unable to comply, the king commanded that all of the wise men should be slain (Daniel 2:13). Daniel and his companions, who had not been in the king's court, were included in the sweeping order.

When the matter was known to Daniel, he requested time of the king and promised that he would give the interpretation of the dream. Then with his three companions, Hananiah, Mishael, and Azariah, Daniel went to prayer to God who alone could reveal the secret. When the dream was made known to Daniel, he recognized the profound character of the divine revelation. His hymn of worship and praise is recorded in Daniel 2:20-23:

> Blessed be the name of God for ever and ever: for wisdom and might are his: And he changeth the times and the seasons: he removeth kings, and setteth up kings: he giveth wisdom unto the wise, and knowledge to them that know understanding: He revealeth the deep and secret things: he knoweth what is in the darkness, and the light dwelleth with him. I thank thee, and praise thee, O thou God of my fathers, who hast given me wisdom and might, and hast made known unto me now what we desired of thee: for thou hast now made known unto us the king's matter.

DANIEL'S DESCRIPTION OF THE DREAM

When brought before the king, Daniel made no claim for insight or wisdom of his own, but declared plainly:

The secret which the king hath demanded cannot the wise men, the astrologers, the magicians, the soothsayers, shew unto the king; But there is a God in heaven that revealeth secrets, and maketh known to the king Nebuchadnezzar what shall be in the latter days (Daniel 2:27, 28).

Daniel then recited the details of Nebuchadnezzar's great dream (Daniel 2:31-35):

Thou, O king, sawest, and behold a great image. This great image, whose brightness was excellent, stood before thee; and the form thereof was terrible. This image's head was of fine gold, his breast and his arms of silver, his belly and his thighs of brass, his legs of iron, his feet part of iron and part of clay. Thou sawest till that a stone was cut out without hands, which smote the image upon his feet that were of iron and clay, and brake them to pieces. Then was the iron, the clay, the brass, the silver, and the gold, broken to pieces together, and became like the chaff of the summer threshingfloors; and the wind carried them away, that no place was found for them: and the stone that smote the image became a great mountain, and filled the whole earth.

FOUR GREAT WORLD EMPIRES

Having declared the dream, Daniel then gave the interpretation. Four great world empires were to succeed each other, to be climaxed by a kingdom which comes from heaven. Nebuchadnezzar was identified as the head of gold, the supreme ruler of the civilized world of his day. Two other kingdoms are mentioned briefly by Daniel in Daniel 2:39, "And after thee shall arise another kingdom inferior to thee, and another third kingdom of brass, which shall bear rule over all the earth." These two kingdoms are represented in the body of the image.

Major attention, however, is directed to the fourth empire as being of supreme, prophetic importance, preceding as it does the final kingdom which comes from God. The fourth kingdom is represented by the legs and feet of the image:

And the fourth kingdom shall be strong as iron: forasmuch as iron breaketh in pieces and subdueth all things: and as iron that breaketh all these, shall it break in pieces and bruise. And whereas thou sawest the feet and toes, part of potters' clay, and part of iron, the kingdom shall be divided; but there shall be in it of the strength of the iron, forasmuch as thou sawest the iron mixed with miry clay. And as the toes of the feet were part of iron, and part of clay, so the king-

dom shall be partly strong, and partly broken. And whereas thou
sawest iron mixed with miry clay, they shall mingle themselves with
the seed of men: but they shall not cleave one to another, even as
iron is not mixed with clay (Daniel 2:40-43).

THE FOURTH EMPIRE

Although the first three kingdoms are clearly identified in Daniel in subsequent chapters, namely, Babylon, Medo-Persia (chapter 5), and Greece (8:21), the fourth kingdom is not named. There
can be little doubt, however, that it refers to the Roman Empire,
the greatest of all the world empires of history and one which had
a larger effect upon subsequent posterity than any of the preceding
empires. Even to modern times, there has never been an empire
equal to that of the ancient Roman Empire.

The description given of it is typical of the Roman Empire. It
is described as "strong as iron" (Daniel 2:40) and as an empire
which breaks in pieces all that opposes it. This is, of course, precisely what the Roman armies did as they swept almost irresistibly
into country after country, first of all conquering the western portion of the empire and then later the eastern portion. Although
the division of the Roman Empire into western and eastern portions did not come until late in its history, it is anticipated in the
fact that the image has two legs.

Major attention, however, is directed to the weakness in the
feet and the toes described in verses 41-43. It is obvious that this
is a matter of major importance. The feet and toes of the image
are described as being part of pottery or clay and part of iron. This
is interpreted as revealing in part its strength and at the same time
its weakness in that the pottery was brittle and easily and quickly
broken. Further, in verse 43 attention is called to the fact that
iron and clay do not adhere one to the other and do not properly
bond.

Whether this difference in material reflects differences in
political ideology such as democracy versus absolute rule, differences in culture or race, or differences in economic situations, it is
clear that the feet of the image are an area of weakness which
leads to its complete downfall. In the light of the prophecy which
follows, the feet stage of the image is best understood to refer to
a form of the Roman Empire which is yet future, namely, the time
just before "the God of heaven" shall "set up a kingdom, which
shall never be destroyed" (2:44).

Many attempts have been made to find in the history of the Roman Empire a stage which corresponds to the toes of the image which may be presumed to be ten in number corresponding to the ten horns of the later vision in Daniel 7:7. It should be observed, first, that this situation demands a period in which the Roman Empire is divided into precisely ten kingdoms. There is no such period in the history of the Roman Empire. Although in its latter stages it was divided up into separate kingdoms, there never was a time when there were precisely ten such kingdoms, and no event followed such as is depicted in Daniel 2:44, 45. For the prophetic vision, therefore, to be completely fulfilled, there must be a future fulfillment.

THE FIFTH KINGDOM FROM HEAVEN

The prophecy of the destruction of the image is embraced in Daniel 2:44, 45:

> And in the days of these kings shall the God of heaven set up a kingdom, which shall never be destroyed: and the kingdom shall not be left to other people, but it shall break in pieces and consume all these kingdoms, and it shall stand for ever. Forasmuch as thou sawest that the stone was cut out of the mountain without hands, and that it brake in pieces the iron, the brass, the clay, the silver, and the gold; the great God hath made known to the king what shall come to pass hereafter: and the dream is certain, and the interpretation thereof sure.

It is clear that the stone cut out of the mountain without hands smites the image on the feet — that is, its last stage — with the result that the entire image is completely destroyed. The destruction cannot be properly compared to the advance of Christianity within the bounds of the ancient Roman Empire; that action was a gradual permeation which never assumed catastrophic character and never vitally changed the political aspect of the Roman Empire. History is clear that the Roman Empire was destroyed not by Christianity, but by its own inherent weaknesses and immorality.

What is demanded in fulfillment of this prophetic interpretation is a sudden catastrophic event which destroys all vestige of Gentile power and replaces it with the kingdom which God Himself establishes. The stone represents a divine agency rather than human, indicated in the fact that it is cut out without hands and is a proper representation of Jesus Christ as the crushing stone of judgment at His second advent. The Christian Gospel to the present hour has never had power to destroy Gentile government in the world and replace it with spiritual government, and there is no prospect that it will. Only divine intervention in the human scene and a display of the omnipotence of God could possibly break up the power of this world and convert it into the kingdom of heaven.

PROPHECY FULFILLED IN HISTORY

The prophetic foreview of world history afforded in the dream of Nebuchadnezzar was remarkably fulfilled except for the consummation. The kingdom of Babylon was indeed the first of the great world empires. Although not the most extensive or powerful in many respects, it was the most glorious. This is anticipated in the gold which represents the Babylonian Empire. After the death of Nebuchadnezzar in 562 B.C., it rapidly deteriorated until on the fateful night described in Daniel 5 on October 13, 539 B.C., Babylon was conquered and the decline of the great city began. The rule of the Medes and the Persians, though less glorious than that of Babylon, was much longer in duration and continued for over two hundred years to 332 B.C. when Alexander the Great conquered Babylon without a battle.

After Alexander's death, the Seleucidae controlled Babylon from 312 to 171 B.C. and were succeeded by the Parthian Empire which successfully resisted Rome and controlled Babylon from 171 B.C. to A.D. 226. Babylon continued to be inhabited in some form or other as late as A.D. 1000. In control of the Holy Land, however, Alexander was succeeded by the Roman Empire. The deterioration in the value of the metals depicted in the image had the compensation of increase in strength, and Rome until the time of the Barbarian invasion was truly characterized by the strength of iron.

As is frequently the case in the Old Testament, the prophecy of Daniel takes no notice of the many years separating the first and second advent of Christ. It anticipates a future empire in the Mediterranean area which will correspond to the ancient Roman Empire and which, from the divine viewpoint, will be a continuation of it. This fourth empire will be succeeded by the kingdom of heaven, begun with a sudden judgment upon Gentile power.

The final world power described in Daniel 2:44, 45 is obviously different in character than the preceding four empires. It is subsequent to these four empires and cannot be brought in until their total destruction. It is a kingdom which is established by the God of heaven rather than by human agency. In contrast to the other empires which had their rise and fall, the kingdom which God establishes will never be destroyed. It shall break in pieces and consume all other powers and shall stand forever.

That the dream was interpreted properly and that the interpretation should be considered factual is brought out in Daniel 2:45 where it is stated: "The great God hath made known to the king what shall come to pass hereafter: and the dream is certain, and the interpretation thereof sure." In the light of the literal and graphic fulfillment of prophecy relating to the first four kingdoms, except for the portion of the fourth which is yet future, it is natural to conclude that the fifth kingdom is also to be literally and factually fulfilled in God's future program.

The grandeur of this panorama of human history and the important place that it assigned the kingdom of Babylon as the first of the succession of world empires so impressed King Nebuchadnezzar that in spite of his high office and absolute rule it is recorded in Daniel 2:46, "Then the king Nebuchadnezzar fell upon his face, and worshipped Daniel, and commanded that they should offer an oblation and sweet odours unto him." King Nebuchadnezzar also gave testimony that the God of Daniel is "a God of gods, and a Lord of kings, and a revealer of secrets, seeing thou couldest reveal this secret." The elevation of Daniel to a prominent place in the government of the Babylonian Empire testifies to the profound impression made upon King Nebuchadnezzar. The experience of Nebuchadnezzar ultimately resulted in his turning to the God of Israel in faith (Daniel 4).

The revelation given in Daniel 2 of world history in its panoramic form constitutes the essential framework for all prophecy related to the nations. Subsequent details in Daniel and elsewhere in Scripture are amplification and added details and explanations. The Scriptures give special emphasis to the latter stage of the fourth empire and concerning this a great body of prophetic Scripture fills in the total picture.

The guidelines, however, for future fulfillment are found in the past. A study of Babylon, Medo-Persia, and Greece, as prophecies relating to them have been fulfilled, provides an important background for that which is yet future. The geographic area of these kingdoms is involved in the final chapters of world history. Babylon has perpetuated itself religiously and to some extent is reproduced politically in the last stage of the fourth kingdom. A study of prophecy relating to these kingdoms as well as historic fulfillment is, then, the Biblical introduction to the nations in the end of the age.

Chapter V

THE RISE AND FALL OF BABYLON

Early History of Babylon

The early history of Babylon is shrouded in mystery. First mentioned in the Bible is the record of Genesis 10:8-10 which names Nimrod, the grandson of Ham, as the founder of the city in the dim prehistoric past. Its name was derived from a later experience revealed in Genesis 11 where the inhabitants of the land of Shinar, the southern portion of Mesopotamia, are recorded as building a tower designed to reach the heavens. This may have been the beginning of a practice of building towers with religious significance. Such a tower is known as a ziggurat, designating an artificial mound of brick and soil elevated above the surrounding terrain.

The Biblical description of the tower is in keeping with the characteristics of the area. Lacking stones, they made brick and used slime or bitumen native to the area in the construction of the tower. According to Scripture, the inhabitants had said,

> Go to, let us make brick, and burn them thoroughly. And they had brick for stone, and slime had they for mortar. And they said, Go to, let us build us a city and a tower, whose top may reach unto heaven; and let us make us a name, lest we be scattered abroad upon the face of the whole earth (Genesis 11:3, 4).

The Scriptures record that the Lord judged the people and confounded their language with the result that the city and the tower were left unfinished (Genesis 11:5-8). The place according to Genesis 11:9 was "called Babel; because the Lord did there confound the language of all the earth: and from thence did the Lord scatter them abroad upon the face of all the earth." It seems probable that the name given to the city in Genesis 10:10 actually supplanted the original name at this time, and this incident contributes to the long history of Babylon as a center of religious significance, and as a source of false religion and rebellion against the true God.

Although the city of Babylon does not rise to prominence until 1830 B.C., the area in which it is located, called Babylonia, had a long history. Early civilization near the site of ancient Ur in lower Babylonia dates from the fourth millennium B.C. and successive civilizations have been traced from 2800 B.C. The period of the early dynasties (2800-2360 B.C.) recorded an advanced civilization including great temples, canals, and other construction. The old Akkadian period (2360-2180 B.C.) included the extensive empire of Sargon from Persia to the Mediterranean. This was followed by the Neo-Sumerian period (2070-1960 B.C.), in which time Abraham was born. The land was sacked by the Elamites and Amorites in the period 1960-1830 B.C.

The history of Babylonia proper, known as the Old Babylonia period (1830-1550 B.C.), included the brilliant reign of Hammurabi (1728-1686 B.C.) whose famous Code was discovered in 1901. Babylonia was next invaded by the Kassites in the period 1550-1169 B.C. This was followed by Dynasty II of Isin (1169-1039 B.C.), whose kings were native Babylonians. In the period from 1100 to 625 B.C. the land suffered various invasions including that of Assyria. In 729 B.C. Tiglath-pileser became king of Babylon and later in 689 B.C. attacked by Sennacherib, Babylon was destroyed by fire. It was rebuilt by Esarhaddon, and was finally wrested from Assyria around 625 B.C. when the Neo-Babylonian Empire was founded by Nabopolassar, the father of Nebuchadnezzar. With the help of the Medes, Nineveh was destroyed in 612 B.C. Necho of Egypt was defeated in 605 B.C. The stage was now set for the brilliant reign of Nebuchadnezzar which included the earlier conquering of Jerusalem in 606 B.C., the ultimate captivity of its inhabitants, and the destruction of the city itself.

THE PROPHECIES OF ISAIAH CONCERNING BABYLON

Apart from a reference to a "Babylonish garment" in Joshua 7:21, there is no Biblical reference to Babylon after Genesis 11 until the great prophecies of Isaiah, Jeremiah, Ezekiel, and Daniel unfolded God's plan for the ancient city. Most of the Biblical prophecies relating to Babylon are in relation to the captivity and God's revelation to Jeremiah, Ezekiel, and Daniel concerning the ultimate end of the captivity both for Israel and for Babylon. Most remarkable, however, are the prophecies of Isaiah delivered a century before Babylon had risen to power and recorded at a time when Babylon was still in obscurity with no indication of its coming greatness. Outstanding chapters in Isaiah's predictions are 13, 14, and 47 with scattered references elsewhere (21:9, 39:1, 3, 6, 7; 43:14; 48:14, 20).

The predictions of Isaiah have to do with Babylon's ultimate destruction in the Day of the Lord. The near and the far view are often mingled as in chapter 13. The destruction of Babylon is pictured in Isaiah 13:1-11 as part of God's program to punish the entire world (cp. 13:11). The historic conquering of Babylon by the Medes and the Persians is mentioned specifically in Isaiah 13: 17-19.

> Behold, I will stir up the Medes against them, which shall not regard silver; and as for gold, they shall not delight in it. Their bows also shall dash the young men to pieces; and they shall have no pity on the fruit of the womb; their eye shall not spare children. And Babylon, the glory of kingdoms, the beauty of the Chaldees' excellency, shall be as when God overthrew Sodom and Gomorrah.

The prophet seems to refer to the far view, that is, the destruction of Babylon in relation to the second coming of Christ in 13: 20-22. Here it is declared:

> It shall never be inhabited, neither shall it be dwelt in from generation to generation: neither shall the Arabian pitch tent there; neither shall the shepherds make their fold there. But wild beasts of the desert shall lie there; and their houses shall be full of doleful creatures; and owls shall dwell there, and satyrs shall dance there. And the wild beasts of the islands shall cry in their desolate houses, and dragons in their pleasant palaces: and her time is near to come, and her days shall not be prolonged.

As far as the historic fulfillment is concerned, it is obvious from both Scripture and history that these verses have not been literally fulfilled. The city of Babylon continued to flourish after the Medes conquered it, and though its glory dwindled, especially after the control of the Medes and Persians ended in 323 B.C., the city continued in some form or substance until A.D. 1000 and did not experience a sudden termination such as is anticipated in this prophecy.

Interpretation has been made more difficult by the varied meanings of Babylon itself. Sometimes the term (in the Hebrew *Babel*) refers to the city whose history continued and was flourishing even during the Apostolic period when it became a center of Jewish learning after the destruction of Jerusalem. Sometimes the term is used in reference to the political power of Babylon which obviously fell in one night when the Medes and the Persians took control of Babylon. Sometimes it is used in a religious sense, for Babylon has been the fountain of many of the pagan religions which have competed with Judaism and Christian faith ever since. The interpretation of Isaiah 13:20-22 is inevitably determined by the meaning assigned to Revelation 17, 18.

Many interpreters agree that Babylon in its religious and political sense will be revived at the end of the age. Debated is the conclusion that the city itself will have a physical revival to become the capital of the world at the end of the age. Such a rebuilding of the ancient city would make possible a literal fulfillment of the prophecy of complete and sudden destruction as predicted in Isaiah 13:19-22.

Isaiah 14 seems to confirm that the ultimate destruction in view is one related to the second advent of Christ and the Day of the Lord. The satanic power behind Babylon addressed as "Lucifer, son of the morning" (14:12) is portrayed both in his original rebellion against God and in his ultimate judgment. The destruction of Babylon is related to the judgment upon "all the kings of the nations" (14:18).

Another massive prophecy against Babylon is found in Isaiah 47. Here a prediction of Babylon's utter humiliation is given, and the foreview seems to relate primarily to the capture of Babylon by the Medes and the Persians. The sad pronouncement is made at the conclusion of the passage, "None shall save thee" (Isaiah 47:15). The major attention given to Babylon in Isaiah's prophecies confirm Babylon's importance in prophecy relating to the nations.

THE PROPHECIES OF JEREMIAH CONCERNING BABYLON

The prophet Jeremiah like Isaiah devotes two long chapters to the prediction of Babylon's ultimate judgment and destruction

(Jeremiah 50, 51). If the prophecies of Isaiah are remarkable for their anticpation of Babylon's rise to power and the captivity of Judah a hundred years before it actually occurred, the prophecies of Jeremiah are notable because they were delivered at the peak of Babylon's power when it seemed most unlikely that the great nation would fall. Babylon is pictured as being punished because of its cruel treatment of Israel (50:17, 18; 51:24, 49).

Practically all of the predictions of Jeremiah seem to relate to the fall of Babylon by the attack of the Medes and the Persians. Only occasionally does there seem to be a reference to a future ultimate destruction as in Jeremiah 51:62-64. The prophecies of Jeremiah predicting the fall of Babylon at the hands of the Medes and the Persians were graphically fulfilled approximately sixty-five years later, as recorded in Daniel 5.

Major attention is devoted to the captivity of Judah in the prophecies of both Jeremiah and Ezekiel. There is almost constant reference to the Babylonian captivity of Judah in Jeremiah beginning in chapter 20; numerous references are also found in Ezekiel. Much of Jeremiah's ministry was to his own generation as he predicted the downfall of Jerusalem and the victory of the Babylonian armies. Jeremiah is seen as the true prophet of God in contrast to the false prophets who had predicted victory over Babylon (cp. Jeremiah 28:1-17). Jeremiah's prophecies were largely ignored. The first copy of his book was destroyed by the king (36:23). Jeremiah himself suffered affliction and imprisonment (37:15—38: 13). With the capture of Jerusalem, the prophecies of Jeremiah were fully vindicated.

Most important were Jeremiah's prophecies concerning the duration of the captivity, designated as seventy years in Jeremiah 25:11 and 29:10. It was this prophecy which was read by Daniel which led to his prayer for the return of the captives to Jerusalem (Daniel 9:2).

A prominent theme of Jeremiah's prophecies were predictions against Egypt in which he anticipated that Nebuchadnezzar would conquer Egypt. As a traditional enemy of Israel, Egypt was thus to experience God's judgment in the form of coming under the power of Babylon. Jeremiah devotes considerable Scripture to this theme, including 43:10-13; 44:30; 46:1-26. In chapter 44 Jeremiah sends a message to the Jews in Egypt in which he predicts that their attempt to escape the power of Babylon would only result in their own destruction.

THE PROPHECIES OF EZEKIEL CONCERNING BABYLON

Ezekiel echoes the prophecies of Jeremiah relating to the Babylonian captivity (Ezekiel 17:12-24) and like Jeremiah predicts the conquering of Egypt (29:18, 19; 30:10-25; 32:1-32). Added is the prediction of the destruction of Tyre in Ezekiel 26:7 - 28:19.

It is obvious from these many passages in the prophets that Babylon occupies a large place in the prophetic program of the Old Testament for the nations surrounding Israel. It is with this context that Daniel the prophet takes up the theme and relates God's dealings with Babylon to His ultimate purpose of bringing all nations into subjection unto the Son of God.

THE PROPHECIES OF DANIEL CONCERNING BABYLON

Daniel's first recognition of Babylon prophetically was in his interpretation of Nebuchadnezzar's dream. Babylon was represented in the great image by the head of gold, and Daniel recognized the importance of Nebuchadnezzar:

> Thou, O king, art a king of kings: for the God of heaven hath given thee a kingdom, power, and strength, and glory. And wheresoever the children of men dwell, the beasts of the field and the fowls of the heaven hath he given into thine hand, and hath made thee ruler over them all. Thou art this head of gold (Daniel 2:37, 38).

After the death of Nebuchadnezzar, Daniel's vision recorded in chapter 7 includes much added revelation. In his description of the first beast which represents Babylon, Daniel states, "The first was like a lion, and had eagle's wings: I beheld till the wings thereof were plucked, and it was lifted up from the earth, and made stand upon the feet as a man, and a man's heart was given to it" (Daniel 7:4).

Babylon was indeed like the lion, the king of beasts, and had eagle's wings like the king of birds. That the wings would be plucked and the beast would stand as a man with a man's heart was the divine portrayal of Nebuchadnezzar's experience in Daniel 4 as well as an anticipation of the ultimate humiliation of the Babylonian rulers in Daniel 5. In Daniel's interpretation of the tree vision of Nebuchadnezzar in Daniel 4, he had predicted Nebuchadnezzar's humiliation in which he suffered seven years of insanity before his reason returned. Nebuchadnezzar was ready then to give praise to God as he does in Daniel 4:2, 3, 34-37. The prophecies of Daniel were meticulously fulfilled.

THE FALL OF BABYLON

The fall of the Babylonian Empire came suddenly when the Medes and the Persians overran the city of Babylon in a night attack in 539 B.C. Prior to this event, the Babylonian Empire had already fallen on evil days. When Nebuchadnezzar died in 562 B.C., he was succeeded by his son Amel-Marduk who was assassinated only two years later. In 560 B.C. Neriglissar took the throne. When he died in 556 B.C. after only four years of reign, he was succeeded by his son who was assassinated shortly after he came to the throne. Nabonidus then assumed power appointing his son Belshazzar as co-ruler. It was this Belshazzar who held the ungodly feast of Daniel 5 and perished at the hands of the Medes and Persians.

At the time of the downfall of the city of Babylon recorded in Daniel 5, the city was still a monument to the genius of Nebuchadnezzar. According to Herodotus, the city was approximately 14 miles square with the Euphrates River bisecting it north and south. Two sets of walls inner and outer protected the city and, according to standards of the day, rendered it safe from attack from without. If Herodotus can be believed, the walls were indeed formidable being 350 feet high and 87 feet thick. Walls also lined the river on either side and 150 gates of solid brass protected the entrances. On the wall were some 250 watchtowers, 100 feet higher than the wall itself. The outside wall had a deep water moat some 30 feet wide.

During the height of its power, provisions were stored in Babylon supposedly sufficient for twenty years of siege and designed to discourage anyone attacking it. Within the walls the city was laid out in square blocks with beautiful houses lining the streets usually three and four stories in height. The city also included great parks and gardens, some of which, such as the hanging gardens described by Diodorus, were outstanding wonders in the ancient world. The gardens were built on terraces and supported large trees. A great bridge some 660 feet long and 30 feet wide bridged the Euphrates River and connected the eastern and western halves of the city. Notable buildings were also found such as the palace of the king, the temple of Bel over eight stories in height, and many other buildings of less importance.

It was this city, proud of its supposed invulnerability, which had ignored the rapidly expanding power of the Medes and the Persians. Media as a separate kingdom had matched the rise of the Babylonian Empire. After the Medes had captured Asshur in 614 B.C. under alliance with the Chaldeans, they had also captured Nineveh. The downfall of the Assyrian Empire, marked by these events, paved the way for the rise in power of Media which was in alliance with Nebuchadnezzar during most of his reign. Persia was also rising in power, however, and under Cyrus II Media was conquered by the Persians about 549 B.C. Media and Persia were united in a common government which lasted until Alexander the Great in 331 B.C. Their armies had proceeded to conquer much of the territory around Babylon before the fateful night in 539 B.C. (Daniel 5).

Setting siege to the large city of Babylon, the Medes had dug a canal diverting the water that flowed under the city wall. At the very time of Belshazzar's impious feast, they were entering the city on the dry channel underneath the mighty walls. The drinking feast celebrated by the one thousand lords apparently was shared by other inhabitants so that the normal watch kept on the walls was not observed, allowing the invaders valuable time in conquering the city before their presence was fully known. At the very time the Medes were pouring into the city, the handwriting appeared on the wall (Daniel 5:5, 24-28). Daniel correctly interpreted the writing as spelling the doom of the Babylonian Empire and the beginning of the empire of the Medes and the Persians (Daniel 5:28, 31). Thus ended the fabulous reign of the Babylonian Empire, the symbol of Gentile glory and moral and religious wickedness.

CONTINUED INFLUENCE OF BABYLON

Although the fall of Babylon marked the end of political rule of Babylonian rulers, much of the Babylonian culture, its pagan religions, and its ideology were continued in the kingdoms which followed. Babylonian influence was perpetuated down through the centuries especially in ancient pagan religions. Babylon, the symbol of religious confusion, was to appear again in the apostate church of Revelation 17, and its political power was to be revived in the final form of the Roman Empire as depicted in Revelation 18. Even if literal Babylon is not rebuilt as a city in the last days and subjected to the sudden destruction described in Revelation 18, Babylon as an influence for evil politically and religiously will not be terminated until Jesus Christ comes in power and glory to reign.

CHAPTER VI

THE MEDES AND THE PERSIANS

The history of the rise and fall of the Medes and the Persians forms an important background for over two hundred years of Biblical history. Located in the area south of the Caspian Sea and east of the Zagros Mountains, its original domain stretched for 600 miles north and south, and 250 miles east to west. The nation first came into prominence in the ninth century B.C. and is mentioned in inscriptions concerning Shalmaneser III (about 836 B.C.). Though under the domination of Assyria until the seventh century B.C., their rise in power was contemporary with the decline of the Assyrian Empire and in 614 B.C. the Medes captured Asshur, the capitol city of Assyria. Later in 612 B.C. in alliance with the Chaldeans they captured Nineveh resulting in the downfall of the Assyrian Empire. In the years which followed they were an important ally of Babylonia and formed various alliances and intermarriages. Toward the end of the reign of Nebuchadnezzar, the Persians began to become a powerful force and under Cyrus II Media was conquered in 549 B.C. and was combined with the empire of the Persians to form Medo-Persia. The combined strength of the Persians and the Medes led to conquest of Babylon in 539 B.C., with the resulting extension of their empire over much of the Middle East until the conquest of Alexander the Great in 331 B.C.

EARLY PROPHECY CONCERNING THE MEDES

First mention of the Medes in Scripture is found in the prophetic utterance of Isaiah when he declared 175 years before it was fulfilled, "Behold, I will stir up the Medes against them, which shall not regard silver; and as for gold, they shall not delight in it" (Isaiah 13:17; cp. 21:2). In succeeding verses the downfall of Babylon is predicted, "And Babylon, the glory of kingdoms, the beauty of the Chaldees' excellency, shall be as when God overthrew Sodom and Gomorrah" (Isaiah 13:19).

70

Jeremiah includes the Medes as one of many nations which will be punished by God (Jeremiah 25:25). Jeremiah also states that the Medes will be used of God to destroy Babylon: "Make bright the arrows; gather the shields: the LORD hath raised up the spirit of the kings of the Medes: for his device is against Babylon, to destroy it; because it is the vengeance of the LORD, the vengeance of his temple" (Jeremiah 51:11; cp. 51:28). Thus long before Babylon fell it was predicted that the Medes would be God's avenging instrument.

PROPHECY OF DANIEL

It was given to Daniel the prophet, however, to give the Medes and the Persians their proper place in the panorama of future history. The Medes and the Persians are anticipated in the expression in Daniel 2:39, "And after thee shall arise another kingdom inferior to thee." This refers to the chest of silver in the image of Daniel 2, where the two arms anticipated the dual kingdom of the Medes and the Persians. More detail is given in the vision of Daniel recorded in 7:5 where Daniel describes the second beast in these words, "And behold another beast, a second, like to a bear, and it raised up itself on one side, and it had three ribs in the mouth of it between the teeth of it: and they said thus unto it, Arise, devour much flesh."

The kingdom of the Medes and the Persians is described as a bear which raises itself on one side (referring to Persia being greater than Media) and has three ribs in its mouth. No explanation is given of this, but the strength of a bear is a good symbol of the empire of the Medes and the Persians. The three ribs may refer to the principal elements of the kingdom, namely, the Medes, the Persians, and Babylonia. The exhortation to "Arise, devour much flesh," is encouragement to the new empire to expand as it did in its conquests to the north and to the west.

A further prophetic picture of the empire of the Medes and the Persians is given in Daniel 8 where the ram with two horns which is destroyed by the goat is an obvious reference to the kingdom of the Medes and the Persians. The two horns represent the Medes and the Persians. Daniel's description of it in Daniel 8:3, 4 is characteristic of the two centuries of the rule of the Medes and the Persians,

> Then I lifted up mine eyes, and saw, and, behold, there stood before the river a ram which had two horns: and the two horns were high;

but one was higher than the other, and the higher came up last. I saw the ram pushing westward, and northward, and southward; so that no beasts might stand before him, neither was there any that could deliver out of his hand; but he did according to his will, and became great.

The lower horn apparently refers to the kingdom of the Medes and the higher horn that came up later to the kingdom of Persia, which dominated Media. The fourth verse describes their conquests westward, northward, and southward which characterize the history of this empire as there was no considerable progress eastward. All of this prediction is precisely fulfilled in later history. Only by divine revelation could Daniel know in advance that the conquests of the Medes and Persians would be to the north, south and west, but not to the east — in contrast to the Macedonian conquests which were mainly to the east, as indicated in subsequent verses in the activities of the he goat.

ISRAEL'S RESTORATION UNDER MEDES AND PERSIANS

While the prophetic record concerning the Medes and the Persians is clear and its fulfillment is confirmed by history, its principal importance is historical rather than prophetic. In contrast to the Babylonian Empire which is significant for its destruction of Jerusalem, the city of God, beginning Gentile dominion over Israel which will not culminate until Christ comes in His second advent, the rise of the Medes and the Persians is important as forming the background of Israel's partial restoration.

Three of the historical books, namely, Ezra, Nehemiah, and Esther and three of the minor prophets, Haggai, Zechariah, and Malachi have their context in the reign of the Medo-Persian Empire. During this period the captives of Judah were permitted to go back to Jerusalem and restore their ancient city and its temple. The key to the Babylonian Empire is Gentile dominion over Jerusalem. The key to the Empire of the Medes and the Persians is restoration of Jerusalem.

Daniel gives a whole chapter to the account of his being cast into the lions' den. This important episode in the life of Daniel, while affording many spiritual lessons of God's care over His prophet as well as foreshadowing God's protection over the people of Israel as a whole, illustrates the beneficent attitude of the Medes and the Persians to the people whom they had conquered. Their deference to individual religious faith is manifested in the attitude of Darius to Daniel and his earnest desire that Daniel might be delivered from the lions.

Darius himself, described in Daniel 5:31 as "Darius the Median," is properly identified as Gobryas or Gubaru, a governor of Babylon appointed by Cyrus the supreme monarch of the empire of the Medes and the Persians. (Cyrus II or Cyrus the Great reigned from 559 B.C. until he was killed in battle in 530 B.C.) Darius the Mede is mentioned a number of times in Daniel (6:1, 6, 9, 25, 28; 9:1; 11:1). Darius seems to have reigned under Cyrus in governing the southern portion of the kingdom known as the Fertile Crescent. The statement that "Daniel prospered in the reign of Darius, and in the reign of Cyrus the Persian" (Daniel 6:28) must therefore be interpreted as the reign of Darius under the contemporary reign of Cyrus.

It was in the first year of the reign of Cyrus that permission was given to the children of Israel to return to reconstruct their temple in Jerusalem (II Chronicles 36:22, 23; Ezra 1:1-4). More than a century before the remarkable prophecy of Isaiah about Cyrus (Isaiah 44:28) had anticipated the Israelites return. The generous permission and encouragement of Cyrus for Israel to restore their ancient worship was in line with the official policy to allow captive people freedom of religion. The temple, however, was not finally completed until the reign of Cambyses II (530-522 B.C.) who succeeded his father Cyrus and is referred to in Ezra 4 as Artaxerxes.

Artaxerxes was a common name ascribed to many kings. Others given this title include Artaxerxes of Ezra 7:1, known as Artaxerxes I Longimanus who reigned 465-425 B.C., and Ahasuerus or Xerxes of Esther 1:1 who reigned 486-465 B.C. The appeal to Darius the king mentioned in Ezra 6:1 is a reference to Darius I, known as Darius the Great who reigned 522-486 B.C., and should not be confused with the Darius the Mede of Daniel's prophecy.

The more important kings of the Medo-Persian Empire are again the subject of prophecy in Daniel 11:2 where Daniel is told: "Behold, there shall stand up yet three kings in Persia; and the fourth shall be far richer than they all: and by his strength through his riches he shall stir up all against the realm of Grecia." The first of the three kings which were to follow Darius the Mede (Daniel 11:1) can be identified as Cambyses II. He was followed by

Smerdis, a usurper who reigned for eight months. (Some think he is the ruler mentioned in Ezra 4:7-24 instead of Cambyses.) After the murder of Smerdis a Darius the Great (522-486 B.C.) appeared. He is referred to in Ezra 4:24. It was under Darius that the authority to complete the temple was received.

The king designated as "the fourth" in Daniel 11:2, who used his great riches to attack the realm of Grecia, was undoubtedly Xerxes (486-465 B.C.) referred to as Ahasuerus in Esther 1:1. His celebrated attempt to conquer Greece ended in miserable failure. This attack can be placed chronologically between the first and the second chapter of Esther. In fact, the great feast of Esther 1 was a part of the preparation for the organization of the campaign against Greece which occurred in the third year of Xerxes' reign. Esther 2, recording his marriage to Esther, did not occur until four years later after his return and the crushing defeat and loss of his great army and naval force. From a prophetic standpoint, Xerxes was important as incurring the undying hatred of the Grecian people which forms the background of the conquest of Alexander the Great more than a century later.

The importance of Ezra, with its record of events which occurred under Persian rule, is that the temple was restored as the center of Israel's religious life. The record of Daniel 8 and 11 is also significant as forming the prophetic bridge from Babylon to Alexander and giving the background of Israel's history in this period. In Ezra 7:1 a successor to Xerxes is mentioned, namely, Artaxerxes I Longimanus, but he does not figure in Daniel's prophecy because he was not important to Daniel's revelation. The same is true of other rulers who followed in the Medo-Persian Empire prior to its downfall.

REBUILDING OF JERUSALEM

Nehemiah adds the important final chapter in Israel's reconstruction. Under Nehemiah's leadership during the reign of Artaxerxes I Longimanus the wall of Jerusalem was rebuilt with the encouragement and supply of materials from the king, and subsequently the debris of the city was cleared out and houses were built, thus repopulating the city of God. The two important steps of rebuilding the temple and rebuilding the city during the reign of the Persians mark this period as the time of Israel's partial restoration in preparation for the coming of their Messiah. The spiritual revivals under Ezra and Nehemiah are a corresponding spiritual restoration which the people thoroughly needed.

The prophetic writings of Haggai and Zechariah also fit into this period and are related to the prophetic encouragement of the people during the reconstruction of the temple of Ezra 5. Malachi gives the concluding chapter of the Old Testament before Israel was plunged into the so-called four hundred silent years before Christ came. The history of the Medes and the Persians, constituting as it does accurate and meticulous fulfillment of God's prophetic Word, is another important evidence supporting the hope that prophecies yet unfulfilled will have their day of fulfillment in the consummation of the age. The Medes and the Persians, however, belong to fulfilled prophecy and do not figure largely in events of the end time although Persia is mentioned in passing in Ezekiel 38:5.

Chapter VII

THE KINGDOM OF GREECE

The third world kingdom, which was to succeed that of the Medes and the Persians, was the empire created by Alexander the Great whose armies were victorious over the Persians in 331 B.C. Only occasional reference to this empire is found by name in the Bible. It does not seem to have attracted the attention of the great prophets Isaiah and Jeremiah, and it does not coincide with Biblical history in that it fits into the period between Malachi and Matthew.

Biblical Background

The Hebrew does not actually use the word for *Greece* or *Grecia,* but the word *yawan* or its English equivalent *javan.* This name is derived from Javan of Genesis 10:2, one of the sons of Japheth and therefore a grandson of Noah. It is commonly believed, however, that Javan was the progenitor of the Greek race which inhabited not only Greece but the islands related to it and hence is properly translated by *Grecian* where it occurs (cp. Isaiah 66:19; Ezekiel 27:13, 19; Daniel 8:21; 10:20; 11:2; Joel 3:6; Zechariah 9:13).

Prophecy of Daniel

According to the prophecy of Daniel in his interpretation of Nebuchadnezzar's image, the Grecian Empire was to be the third kingdom of brass (Daniel 2:39). Further light on the characteristics of this empire is given in Daniel 7:6 in the description of the third beast of Daniel's vision. Daniel describes the third beast as "like a leopard, which had upon the back of it four wings of a fowl; the beast had also four heads; and dominion was given to it." While Daniel's prophecies concerning Nebuchadnezzar and the kingdom of the Medes and the Persians were fulfilled in part in Daniel's lifetime, in his prediction of the empire of Greece he accurately foreshadowed an empire which did not come into existence until two hundred years later. It would have been impossible for Daniel by any natural insight to have anticipated that a small and insignificant Greek state, namely, Macedonia, should reach such great power and prestige and have such a rapid rise as that of Alexander's kingdom.

CONQUESTS OF ALEXANDER THE GREAT

History records how Alexander with the agility of a goat crossed the Hellespont, having previously conquered Greece, and began the march to revenge the humiliation inflicted upon Greece by Xerxes more than a century before. Conquering Troy, he first met Persian opposition at Granicus and after subduing all of Asia Minor proceeded to battle a host of one-half million Persians whom Darius had assembled. Meeting in the plain of Issus, he slaughtered the greatly superior Persian force and broke the back of Persian opposition. Proceeding southward, city after city yielded without a fight except for Tyre and Gaza where a siege was necessary before it was subdued.

Continuing south to Egypt, Alexander conquered the entire country without a fight and established the city Alexandria as the capital of the area, which soon became the largest city of the Hellenic world. Proceeding east he had still another battle with Darius at Issus and again defeated a greatly superior force. His armies reached India, but his troops, weary with battle, refused to go further.

Returning to Babylon, Alexander intended to make this the capital of his entire empire. While engaged in establishing his new organization, he died a victim of his profligate eating and drinking coupled with an attack of malaria. Brief as was his domain, the fact that he carried Greek culture with him and often established new cities on a Hellenic pattern had the effect of leaving his mark upon the civilized world of his day and indirectly prepared the area of his conquest to receive the Gospel later which was largely preached in Greek. The extent of his conquest is all the more remarkable because it was foreshadowed in such a clear way in Biblical prophecy.

The description of the leopard, one of the swiftest of beasts, characterizes the lightning-like attack of Alexander's armies which with unprecedented speed swept the world of his day into its power. The four wings on the back of the leopard not only represent the idea of speed, but also symbolize the historic fact that Alexander's empire was controlled after his death by four principal generals, also, anticipated in the four heads of the beast. The accuracy of this prophecy is so evident that liberal scholars who consider detailed prophecy an impossibility are forced to postulate that the entire book of Daniel is in fact a forgery written by a pseudo-Daniel who lived after these events of Alexander's conquest had already taken place. This unwilling confession of the accuracy of Biblical prophecy is in itself most significant and a testimony to the accuracy of prophecy as a whole.

THE PROPHECY OF DANIEL 8

Unlike the kingdoms of Babylon and that of Media and Persia, there is little prophecy concerning Alexander and his empire outside of Daniel. It does not seem to have attracted the attention of any of the other prophets, although bare mention is made as previously indicated. More detail is given in Daniel about the Alexandrian Empire, however, than any of the preceding kingdoms. The entire eighth chapter is devoted to portraying the rise of the third empire and further details are given in chapter 11.

In a vision given to Daniel before the fall of Babylon, the conquest of the kingdom of the Medes and the Persians by Alexander was depicted in the destruction of the ram with two horns by the goat with the important horn between its eyes. After describing the conquest of the ram, which portrays the power of the kingdom of the Medes and the Persians, Daniel records the destruction of the Persian Kingdom by Alexander in these words:

> And as I was considering, behold, an he goat came from the west on the face of the whole earth, and touched not the ground: and the goat had a notable horn between his eyes. And he came to the ram that had two horns, which I had seen standing before the river, and ran unto him in the fury of his power. And I saw him come close unto the ram, and he was moved with choler against him, and smote the ram, and brake his two horns: and there was no power in the ram to stand before him, but he cast him down to the ground, and stamped upon him: and there was none that could deliver the ram out of his hand (Daniel 8:5-7).

This description accurately predicted the conquest of the Persian Empire by Alexander and his armies which brought to a close more than two hundred years of the illustrious political power under the Persians. The interpretation of these verses is plainly given in Daniel 8:20, 21, "The ram which thou sawest having two horns are the kings of Media and Persia. And the rough goat is the king of Grecia: and the great horn that is between his eyes is the first king."

DIVISION OF GRECIAN EMPIRE

As history records, however, Alexander the Great, while able to conquer the world, was not able to conquer himself. When at the pinnacle of his power, Alexander died in a drunken feast and his conquests were peaceably divided between his four generals. This is anticipated in Daniel 8:8: "Therefore the he goat waxed very great: and when he was strong, the great horn was broken; and for it came up four notable ones toward the four winds of heaven." This is interpreted in Daniel 8:22 as being the four kingdoms into which the Grecian Empire was divided, headed up by the four generals of Alexander. Ptolemy was given Egypt and adjacent territories. To Seleucas was given Syria, Asia Minor, and the East. Lysimachus took control of Thrace and adjoining territories. Cassander ruled over Macedonia and Greece itself. Eventually Macedonia and Thrace were joined, resulting in the emergence of three strong kingdoms, Macedonia, Syria, and Egypt. Political rule was therefore divided until the Roman Empire arose to provide a new unifying political factor.

ANTIOCHUS EPIPHANES

Daniel is primarily concerned in his prophetic foreview in Daniel 8 with what constituted a relatively unimportant aspect of the total picture from the standpoint of world history, but what was to be quite important in its relationship to the people of Israel. In Daniel 8:9-14, Daniel records the emergence of "a little horn, which waxed exceeding great, toward the south, and toward the east, and toward the pleasant land."

The subsequent description of the little horn indicates that it is a man who opposes God (8:10), exalts himself in opposition to God, and takes away the daily sacrifice (8:11, 12). A question is then raised in Daniel 8:13 as to how long the desolation of the sanctuary shall continue and is answered in 8:14, "Unto two thousand and three hundred days; then shall the sanctuary be cleansed." The vision is subsequently interpreted to Daniel and the revelation is recorded in Daniel 8:15-26. Daniel is informed that the

vision relates to "the time of the end" (8:17). Similar expressions
are found in 8:19, "the last end of the indignation" and "the time appointed the end" (8:19), and "in the latter time of their kingdom,
when the transgressors are come to the full" (8:23). In the interpretation, the ram with the two horns is stated to be "the kings of Media
and Persia" (8:20), and the rough goat is stated to be "the king
of Grecia" (8:21). The great horn of the rough goat is declared
to be "the first king" (8:21). According to 8:22, the four horns
which replaced the single broken horn are "four kingdoms" which
shall appear, but which shall not have the power of the great horn.

The little horn of 8:9 is described in 8:23, 24 as "a king of fierce
countenance, and understanding dark sentences" whose "power
shall be mighty, but not by his own power: and he shall destroy
wonderfully, and shall prosper, and practise, and shall destroy the
mighty and holy people." He is described also as opposing the
Prince of princes, but it is declared that "he shall be broken without hand" (8:25). Students of prophecy have recognized in this
description first of all the anticipation of an immediate fulfillment
in connection with the Macedonian Empire.

The most probable interpretation of this little horn is that it
concerns Antiochus Epiphanes, a ruler in the kingdom of Syria
about 170 B.C. His terrible persecution of the Jews which inspired
the Maccabean revolt is a matter of history. Through his instru-
mentality the sacrifices of the Jews were stopped and their temple
desecrated. With an army of some 22,000 men he attacked Jerusalem on a Sabbath day massacring the men and making captives
of the women and children. He issued a decree commanding that
all should worship only according to the religion of the prevailing
political power. The resulting revolt of the Jewish people was
ultimately resolved only after long struggle and by the ascendance
of the Roman Empire.

The reference to 2300 days (literally 2300 mornings and evenings) is best understood as 2300 ordinary days, during which the
sanctuary remained desecrated. Historically it was approximately
this length of time before a restoration was accomplished. It has
been computed that the sanctuary was cleansed on December 25,
165 B.C. by Judas Maccabaeus. This will allow a period from 171
B.C. to 165 B.C. as the period of desecration. However, as the altar
was not actually desecrated until December 168 B.C., some have
suggested the twenty-three days were actually 1150 mornings plus

1150 evenings, i.e., 2300 mornings and evenings together or approximately 3½ years. In any case, there is no excuse for the interpretation that the 2300 days are years and that this marks the year A.D. 1844 as a prophetic date as one cult has taught. An adequate explanation is found in a literal rendering of this period of time. It is, therefore, properly considered a reference to an important and heroic chapter in Israel's history which is probably the most significant event during the period in which Alexander's successors rule as history is viewed from a Biblical standpoint.

ANTIOCHUS THE FORESHADOWING OF THE FUTURE PRINCE

Many consider the desecration of the Jewish temple by Antiochus Epiphanes a foreshadowing of a still future desecration that will be fulfilled in the time of the great tribulation (cp. Daniel 9:27; Matthew 24:15-22). The references in the interpretation to "the end" and the description given of the king seem in some respects to go beyond Antiochus Epiphanes. In this case the description would apply to the ultimate world ruler previously described in the little horn of Daniel 7 and concerning whom further revelation is given in Revelation 13:1-10. If so, this is another instance of dual fulfillment of prophecy, the partial fulfillment foreshadowing the ultimate fulfillment.

PROPHECIES OF DANIEL 10, 11

Further detail and amplification of this period is found in the remarkable prophecies recorded in Daniel 10, 11. A whole chapter, Daniel 10, is devoted to the introduction in which Daniel is informed that the angelic messenger had been engaged in conflict with demonic powers for three weeks and thus delayed in bringing his message to Daniel (cp. Daniel 10:13). Daniel then records in Daniel 11:1-35 one of the most detailed prophecies to be found anywhere in the Word of God. It has been estimated that one hundred thirty-five prophecies are contained in these thirty-five verses and that all of these prophecies have already been fulfilled.

Details concerning the persecutions of Antiochus Epiphanes are given in Daniel 11:21-35. Most of the passage describes his conflict with Egypt, "the king of the south." Antiochus himself is described as "a vile person, to whom they shall not give the honour of the kingdom: but he shall come in peaceably, and obtain the kingdom by flatteries" (Daniel 11:21).

At the height of his power he was forced by the rising power of the Roman Empire to give up Egypt. Turning his attention to his own land, he began the persecution of the Jews as previously described in Daniel 8:11-14. In the process it is declared, "They shall pollute the sanctuary of strength, and shall take away the daily sacrifice, and they shall place the abomination that maketh desolate" (Daniel 11:31). The persecution of Israel is indicated in the words, "they shall fall by the sword, and by flame, by captivity, and by spoil, many days" (Daniel 11:33). This is an accurate description of the terrors of the Maccabean persecutions.

After describing the role of Antiochus the prophecy leaps to the end of the age in Daniel 11:36 to describe "the king" who "shall do according to his will." This is probably a reference to the final world ruler of whom Antiochus Epiphanes is a foreshadowing. The portion of the prophecy already fulfilled has had its graphic realization in history and stands as another testimony to the accuracy of the prophetic Word. The prophetic vision of Daniel, beginning in verse 36 of the chapter, still remains to be fulfilled in the time of great tribulation of which the trials and persecutions of Antiochus Epiphanes were an anticipation.

GRECIAN EMPIRE A PREPARATION FOR ROME

The precise fulfillment of prophecy in the Grecian Empire sets the stage for the fourth and final Gentile world power, that of Rome, which dominated the scene at the time Christ was born in Bethlehem. It is this empire which figures largely in the history of the church as well as in prophecy of things to come and constitutes the framework of prophecy related to the nations in the end of the age.

Chapter VIII

THE RISE AND FALL OF ROME

Long before Antiochus Epiphanes had fulfilled the prophecies of Daniel 8:23-25 and 11:21-35, the fourth empire of Daniel's prophecy was already in the making in the rising power of Rome. Roman power was manifested first in the conquering of Italy except for the far north. Rome then proceeded to challenge Carthage which at that time was the absolute master of all Northern Africa. Carthage had been founded by Phoenicians from Tyre and Sidon centuries before, but in the divided power of the Macedonian Empire it was possible for Carthage not only to conquer Northern Africa, but many islands in the Mediterranean including Sicily.

The expanding power of Rome was first manifested in conquering Sicily in 242 B.C., and Carthage had to recognize this conquest in the following year. Although Carthage continued to meet success in conquering Spain and under Hannibal made remarkable progress in extending its power into Gaul, these victories were short lived. It was not long until Rome attacked Spain, and in 202 B.C. at the battle of Zama in North Africa Carthage came under Roman control as a tributary and was eventually destroyed completely in 146 B.C.

The Rise of Roman Power

With the beginning of the second century B.C., the western Mediterranean became a Roman lake. The Roman Empire also extended in the north to the Alps, but the next major move was to the east. One by one the nations fell, first Macedonia, then Greece, then Asia Minor. Countries conquered were often allowed to have local government for a time which later would be replaced by Roman rulers. The prophetic description of Rome as a monster with great iron teeth which trod underfoot its opponents (Daniel 7:7) was fulfilled again and again. People seized in conquered countries were sold by the hundreds and thousands, and all menial tasks were performed by these slaves. Such was the power of Rome that Antiochus Epiphanes who had previously been compelled to surrender Egypt to Rome barely survived the threat of Roman domination until his death in 164 B.C., but thereafter Syria also became Roman. Roman conquest continued with the conquering of Palestine under the Roman general Pompeius who subdued Jerusalem in 63 B.C. Thus it was that our Lord was born in Bethlehem where Joseph had gone in obedience to a Roman order for registration.

Meanwhile Roman power was being extended throughout middle Europe including what is today Great Britain, Switzerland, France, and Belgium, with all the territory south of the Rhine and the Danube in Roman hands as well as some territory to the north. The march of Rome continued until by the end of the second century A.D. most of Mesopotamia and the area up to the Euphrates River was under Roman control. Everywhere as country after country fell under the heel of Rome, thousands were carried off into slavery and extreme brutality became the order of the day.

The glory of Rome was built on the misery of its conquered peoples. Thus were the prophecies of the fourth kingdom accurately fulfilled as in Daniel 2:40, "And the fourth kingdom shall be strong as iron: forasmuch as iron breaketh in pieces and subdueth all things: and as iron that breaketh all these, shall it break in pieces and bruise." Daniel's prophecies thus far have been graphically fulfilled in history.

PROPHESIED END OF ROME NOT FULFILLED

It is essential to the understanding of prophecy relating to the fourth empire to discern, however, that the final state of this empire described in Daniel 2:42-45 has never been fulfilled. In like manner, the description of the beast as having ten horns and the further development of the emergence of a little horn by which three of the first horns were uprooted (Daniel 7:7, 8) has never been fulfilled. It is also evident that there has been no literal fulfillment of the fifth kingdom which was to succeed the fourth, namely, the kingdom described as that of the Son of Man which is everlasting in its character and which can only come when the fourth kingdom is destroyed.

In contrast to the first three beasts who according to Daniel 7:12 "had their dominion taken away: yet their lives were prolonged for a season and time," the fourth beast according to Daniel 7:11 "was slain, and his body destroyed, and given to the burning flame." The fourth beast according to these prophecies was violently and dramatically to be broken at the time of the institution of the kingdom given to the Son of Man.

THE FALL OF ROME IN HISTORY

Nothing should be clearer from the subsequent history of the Roman Empire than that there has been no fulfillment of this last stage of the Roman Empire. The growth of the Roman Empire took almost four centuries, in contrast to the rapid rise of the three preceding empires. It was also slow to disintegrate.

As the history of the Roman Empire makes clear, the western half from which its power originated was the first to go down. The details of this need only be mentioned in a general way. It began with the division of the empire into the eastern and western parts in A.D. 364 by the Emperor Valentinian I. In the fifth century, barbarians from the north such as the Goths, originating in northeastern Germany, conquered most of southwestern Europe and a large part of Spain. Much of France was also occupied and Roman troops had to leave Great Britain as early as A.D. 409.

Eventually the barbarians invaded Italy itself and, under Attila, the Huns not only conquered much of Europe, setting up a rival kingdom to the eastern half of the Roman Empire, but invaded Italy in A.D. 451. Italy was also attacked by the Vandals and Moors in A.D. 455 who invaded Italy by sea from North Africa, taking off many of the objects of wealth to Carthage, including the vessels from the temple at Jerusalem captured by Titus in A.D. 70. All of these tremendously significant movements in Europe and in North Africa tended to wrest power from the western half of the Roman Empire.

It is most important, however, to note that none of these movements correspond in the slightest to what the Scriptures anticipate as the last stage of the Roman Empire, namely, the ten nations anticipated in the ten horns of Daniel 7:7 or in the toes of the image in Daniel 2:42. Even if they had, it would not have provided any explanation of the continuance of the eastern half of the Roman Empire, which from a Biblical standpoint was probably more important, inasmuch as it related to the Holy Land.

The destruction of the Roman Empire in its eastern division

was accomplished only after the western Roman Empire had been practically destroyed. This was effected largely by the rising tide of the followers of Mohammed (A.D. 570-632) who had as their goal the conquering of the eastern aspect of the empire. After the death of Mohammed, his successor conquered Persia. Later leaders gained control over Syria, Palestine, and Egypt, extending their power over all of North Africa and into Spain. The rapid rise of the empire of the followers of Mohammed, however, lacked a cohesive force and soon various portions of it declared their independence.

The political weakness of Mohammedanism paved the way for the conquest of the Turks who had originally come from Central Asia. The Turks rapidly conquered Persia, Armenia, and Asia Minor. Although opposed by the Crusaders who attempted to conquer Palestine and free it from the Turks as well as the Saracens (followers of Mohammed), the Turks, nevertheless, although opposed by the Mongols in the thirteenth century, consolidated their power in Asia Minor. Under the Ottomans, they succeeded in conquering all the area around the Black Sea including Constantinople and Greece, as well as Northern Africa and Egypt, also extending their power into the Mesopotamia valley.

In A.D. 1453 Mohammed II conquered Constantinople, installing Moslem worship. In the process, the Roman Empire, for all practical purposes, ceased to exist with the death of the last of the Roman emperors who was killed in the battle. The decline of the Turkish Empire began shortly before the seventeenth century, but in the twentieth century they still controlled Asia Minor, the Holy Land, and the Mesopotamian valley. One of the important results of World War I was the freeing of the Holy Land from Turkish domination.

THE FUTURE DESTRUCTION OF ROME

It should be evident from this brief historical survey that nothing corresponding to the complete destruction of the image of Daniel 2 or the beast of Daniel 7 occurred in the gradual deterioration of the Roman Empire. More than 1,500 years elapsed from the beginning of the Roman Empire to its final complete destruction, A.D. 1453. A more gradual process could hardly be imagined, nor is it true that the empire was destroyed by Christians or by the power of the Gospel as some postmillenarians teach. Rather, the normal courses of war and superior military might took its toll. With its decline the Roman Empire left unfulfilled that of which prophecy had spoken, namely, the sudden destruction of the feet stage of the image of Daniel 2 and the ten-horn stage of the beast of Daniel 7:7.

Inasmuch as the first portion of the prophecy concerning the Roman Empire was so graphically fulfilled in history just as other prophecies relating to the preceding empires of Babylon, Medo-Persia, and Greece, it is most reasonable to conclude that the final stage of the Roman Empire will also have its precise fulfillment. At that future time the stage will be set for its complete destruction and the bringing in of the fifth kingdom, by the Son of Man, which will occur at the second coming of Christ.

Chapter IX

THE REVIVAL OF ROME

The Middle East the Center of World History

For careful students of history the possibility of revival of the ancient Roman Empire has long been considered plausible. The history of the world for the last 2,500 years has had its principal center of interest in Southern Europe, Northern Africa, and Western Asia. It is only in the last millennium that Northern Europe and Great Britain have become principal actors, and still more recent is the rise of power in the United States of America. While world population in Asia has always exceeded the population of the other continents, somehow they have not figured as largely in the major events of the last millennium.

The Middle East as the geographic hub of three major continents is by its location as well as its long history destined to play an important part in the future. Predictions are not wanting even from non-Christian writers that the Middle East would once again in the future be the center of world political and economic interest. In such a context the revival of the ancient Roman Empire does not seem to be as unlikely as would first appear.

Unfulfilled Prophecy Concerning the Times of Gentiles

For the Biblical expositor, however, the principal reason for believing in the revival of the ancient Roman Empire is the fact that prophecies dealing with the latter part of this empire have not been fulfilled, in contrast to the specific and detailed fulfillment which occurred in connection with the first three empires — Babylon, Medo-Persia, and Greece — and the first stage of the fourth empire of Rome. Inasmuch as fulfillment of the first portion of this prophecy concerning the times of the Gentiles has been so minute, as illustrated for instance in Daniel 11:1-35, it is logical to assume that the latter portion of the prophecy will have a similar fulfillment. It is for this reason that careful expositors, who fully honor the Word of God as an infallible record and who assume therefore that prophecies of the future are just as authentic as records of history, have concluded that there is yet to appear on the stage of world history a revival of the ancient Roman Empire in the form anticipated in unfulfilled prophecy relating to the times of the Gentiles. The anticipated revival of Rome is related, first, to its geography, second, to indications of its political character, and, third, relationship of the political revival to the last form of apostate religion which will appear before the second advent of Christ.

Geographically the ancient Roman Empire at the height of its power extended from the Euphrates River to the east across Northern Africa and Southern Europe and included a portion of Great Britain. It is obviously not necessary in contemplating such a revival to require that all of this territory should be incorporated in the revived empire in its first stage. It is reasonable to assume, however, that the revived empire would include the ancient capital, Rome, and would be located in a portion of the territory once under Roman control.

THREE FUTURE STAGES OF THE ROMAN EMPIRE

As far as it is possible to understand the prophetic foreview of this revived empire, it appears that geographically it will go through three stages. First, there will appear a confederacy of ten kingdoms within the ancient Roman Empire which will constitute the first phase of its revival. Second, there will appear a strong man who will consolidate these ten nations into a united kingdom and probably extend its borders in various directions. Third, there is the final stage of the Roman Empire when its power extends to the entire earth. The final or third stage may be in a state of partial disintegration at the time of the second coming of Christ as indicated by the very fact that there is warfare and rebellion against the Roman ruler.

THE FUTURE TEN-NATION CONFEDERACY

The Scriptural background for these conclusions is found first in Daniel 2:41-43 where the feet-and-toes stage of the image is described. The Roman Empire, previously divided into eastern and western divisions as indicated by the legs of the image, in its last stage will be represented by the feet of the image, which is divided into ten kingdoms represented by the ten toes, assuming that the toes of the image correspond to the characteristics of man. Daniel chapter 2 does not specifically state that there are ten toes.

The corresponding revelation given in Daniel 7:7, 8 is to some extent more specific and has the advantage of the divine commentary in Daniel 7:17-27 which interprets the characteristics of the fourth beast. The final stage of the Roman Empire is clearly defined in the expression, "it had ten horns" (Daniel 7:7). This is interpreted in Daniel 7:24 as ten kings, "And the ten horns out of this kingdom are ten kings that shall arise."

There have been many attempts to identify these ten nations specifically, but the Scriptures do not give sufficient information. In the study of prophecy it is well on the one hand to take seriously what the Scriptures do reveal, and on the other hand to respect the silence of Scripture. The identity of the nations has not been revealed and with this we may be content. The probability is, however, that the ten nations will include not only portions of Southern Europe and Northern Africa, but also some nations in Western Asia, inasmuch as the revived Roman Empire to some extent is viewed as including the three preceding empires which were largely Asiatic. As the Holy Land is the center of Biblical interest, it would only be natural for the empire to include this area, especially when it is taken into consideration that the Holy Land becomes a part of the area of influence of the Roman Empire as demonstrated in the covenant with Israel (Daniel 9:27) and in the later warfare described as being in this area (Ezekiel 38, 39; Daniel 11:40-45; Zechariah 14:1-3).

Although the identity of the ten nations cannot be determined, there has been much speculation concerning the materials which form the toes of the image described in Daniel 2:41-43 as being partly of iron and partly of pottery or dried clay. In the prophecy attention is called to the fact that iron does not mix with the clay and therefore that the feet of the image are the weakest portion of the entire structure. According to Daniel 2:41, 43, "the toes of the feet were part of iron, and part of clay, so the kingdom shall be partly strong, and partly broken. And whereas thou sawest iron mixed with miry clay, they shall mingle themselves with the seed of men: but they shall not cleave one to another, even as iron is not mixed with clay."

It is clear that inasmuch as the legs of iron represent the strength of the ancient Roman Empire further described in the "great iron teeth" of Daniel 7:7 the clay must in some sense be an area of political weakness. A common interpretation is that the clay is democracy in contrast to the absolute government of the Roman Empire. This, however, seems to be a superficial conclusion as the Roman Empire had during a portion of its history at least a form of democracy.

Another suggestion has been that the clay represents the people of Israel who by their religious and racial characteristics are not easily absorbed in a Gentile government and constitute a difficulty rather than a strength within the revived Roman Empire. This again, however, is conjecture and not without its difficulties.

Probably a safe interpretation is that the clay mixed with iron represents the diverse elements, whether they be racial, religious, or political, that are included in the confines of the revived Roman Empire and contribute to its ultimate downfall. This view may be supported by the fact that the Roman Empire when it does reach its world stage immediately begins to encounter difficulties that result in the final world conflict which is underway when Christ returns. Again it is difficult to be specific where the Word of God does not give us the precise interpretation of the symbolism involved in the clay. The revelation of the fourth empire in Daniel 7 does not mention this weakness.

THE COMING ROMAN PRINCE

That the ten-nation confederacy is a Roman confederacy and a revival of the Roman Empire is brought out in the second stage of the development, not mentioned in Daniel 2, but is revealed in Daniel 7:8. Here according to the Scriptures, out of the ten horns or the original ten kings who formed the first phase of the Roman confederacy another little horn appears representing a ruler who conquers three of the kings and apparently secures the subjection of the others: "I considered the horns, and, behold, there came up among them another little horn, before whom there were three of the first horns plucked up by the roots: and, behold, in this horn were eyes like the eyes of man, and a mouth speaking great things" (Daniel 7:8).

As the prophecy indicates, the little horn is described as a man in that he has eyes like the eyes of a man and a mouth speaking great things such as a man would speak. In the interpretation of the vision in Daniel 7:24 he is described in the words, "Another shall rise after them; and he shall be diverse from the first, and he shall subdue three kings." It is quite obvious that this character is a man who conquers three of the kings by war with the implication that the others submit to him. His blasphemous character is indicated in Daniel 7:25 and his destruction will occur at the second advent in Daniel 7:26, 27.

The fact that he is a Roman prince is a deduction from Daniel 9:26, 27. According to this Scripture in the chronology of Daniel's seventy-sevens of years, the Messiah was to be cut off in the interval between the sixty-ninth seven and the seventieth seven. This refers, of course, to the death of Christ. The prophecy continues, "And the people of the prince that shall come shall destroy the city and the sanctuary" (Daniel 9:26). The most sensible interpretation of this reference is that it concerns the destruction of Jerusalem under the Roman general Titus in A.D. 70 which also occurred in the interval between the sixty-ninth seven and the beginning of the seventieth seven.

The peculiar expression "the people of the prince that shall come" must be interpreted as referring to the Roman people for they were the ones who destroyed the city. It then follows that "the prince that shall come" is also Roman. Inasmuch as he is able to make the political covenant because of his political power, it follows that if he is Roman, then the empire also is Roman. This is, of course, confirmed by the very continuity of the fourth empire linking the last stage with the first stage which was obviously Roman.

As the destruction of Jerusalem came approximately forty years after the Messiah was cut off, it demonstrates clearly that the last seven years of Daniel 9:27 in which a covenant is made with the people of Israel must be subsequent to the destruction of Jerusalem. Therefore, the chronology requires a time period between the sixty-ninth seven and the seventieth seven which has extended to the present day. The prophecy of Daniel 9:27 can only be fulfilled when the Roman prince appears who will make the covenant and when he is in a postion of power to do so. It would therefore follow that the covenant will be signed only after the little horn of Daniel 7 has conquered the ten kings and has reached a place of political supremacy over them. The revival of Israel in the form

of the Israeli nation in the twentieth century may be a preparation
for the fulfillment of this prophecy and one of the indications that
world history may be moving into its final stage.

The possibility of the formation of such a ten-nation confederacy headed by a dictator in the form of "the prince that shall come"
has long been predicted by students of prophecy. Until the period
following World War II, however, humanly speaking it seemed a
remote possibility, although there had been forerunners of such an
idea. As early as 1914, a committee was formed for the promotion
of a European Federation which anticipated political, economic,
and legal ties. The movement toward such a European Federation
emerged after World War I in the League of Nations, an organization which failed, however, to gain sufficient support to endure.

With World War II, and its reminder to the nations of the
world that war is not the best way to settle disputes, the United
Nations was formed, thus embodying for the first time a world
government in principle.

More significant, however, to the possibility of a revival Roman
Empire was the emergence of the European Common Market.
Under agreements between the principal nations of continental
Europe, a gradual reduction in tariffs was achieved, allowing a free
flow of goods from one country to another and unhindered trans-
fer of available labor. The resulting prosperity of Europe under
this arrangement has brought forth many predictions of an ultimate
United States of Europe which could eventually include not only
Europe itself, but the Mediterranean world. Whether the Common
Market in its present form is prophetically significant or not, it si-
lences critics of the idea of a revived Roman Empire who had previously claimed that such a union was impossible because of the
diverse political, economic, and racial factors which had separated
the European nations for centuries. With the economic feasibility
of such a union already demonstrated, it is a relatively short step
to a common banking system and political ties which would bind
various nations together while allowing them freedom on a larger
scale than that afforded by the individual states of the United States
of America.

How the ten-nation confederacy will arise is too early to predict. Many prophecies anticipate that nations will find themselves
in distress and perplexity at the end of the age (cp. Luke 21:25, 26).
The beast of Revelation 13:1 is said to come up out of the sea, a

figure often used of the nations of the world as in Isaiah's prophecy in Isaiah 17:12, 13, where the rushing of the nations is compared to the rushing of mighty waters. The empire will be the child of its times, a result of political, economic, and military pressures.

THE WORLD EMPIRE OF ROME

The final state of the revived Roman Empire politically is described as being an empire which embraces the entire world. This third stage in development is brought out specifically in Daniel 7:23 where the fourth beast is predicted to "devour the whole earth, and shall tread it down, and break it in pieces." This picture of world-wide dominion is confirmed by the companion prophecy found in Revelation 13. Here it is specifically said of the beast that "power was given him over all kindreds, and tongues, and nations. And all that dwell upon the earth shall worship him" (Revelation 13:7, 8).

This final stage where the Roman Empire becomes a world empire is most naturally understood to coincide with the beginning of the great tribulation, a term referring to the last three and one-half years leading up to the second advent of Christ. The Scriptures do not directly explain how the Roman Empire becomes a world empire, but a plausible explanation may be found in the battle of Gog and Magog described in Ezekiel 38, 39.

Here is predicted the destruction of the northern kingdom which apparently challenged the Roman Empire by attacking Israel. With the northern kingdom destroyed there is no major political force standing in the way of the Roman Empire, and the world empire is achieved by proclamation. The apparent invincibility of the Roman ruler, supported as he is by Satanic power, is intimated in the question of Revelation 13:4, "Who is like unto the beast? who is able to make war with him?"

The fact that this world empire begins at the mid-point in Daniel's last seven years leading up to the second advent is supported by Revelation 13:5 where it states that "power was given unto him to continue forty and two months." Inasmuch as the power of this character is broken by the second advent of Christ, it fixes the beginning of his world empire as exactly forty-two months prior to the second advent.

The political character of this world empire is such, however, that it is not firmly established. This paves the way for rebellion of major sections of the world described as leading up to the battle of the great day of God almighty, a world conflict which is brought to an abrupt close by the second coming of Christ and destruction of the contending armies (Revelation 19:11-21).

THE WORLD RELIGION OF ROME

The geographic and political characteristics of the revived Roman Empire form the background for the religious character of the revival of Rome. According to prophetic Scriptures which describe the religious character of the period preceding the second advent of Christ, two major phases can be observed. The first is the apostate church described under the symbolism of the wicked woman of Revelation 17. The present theological apostasy which has engulfed so large a segment of the professing church will in that day, after the true church has been raptured, become a part of the world church movement and apparently will be successful in combining all the unsaved remnant of the professing church left behind at the rapture into a gigantic ecclesiastical organization of tremendous wealth, prestige, and political importance.

The Apostle John was introduced to this ecclesiastical organization symbolized by the woman in Revelation 17. He was invited by the angel, "Come hither; I will shew unto thee the judgment of the great whore that sitteth upon many waters: With whom the kings of the earth have committed fornication, and the inhabitants of the earth have been made drunk with the wine of her fornication" (Revelation 17:1, 2). John thus carried by the Spirit into the wilderness according to Revelation 17:3 beheld the woman who is described as sitting "upon a scarlet coloured beast, full of names of blasphemy, having seven heads and ten horns" (Revelation 17:3).

The beast thus described as blasphemous is unquestionably the same as that in Revelation 13:1 which has seven heads and ten horns and "the name of blasphemy." This beast is the revived Roman Empire in its political character as it will appear in the end of the age. The fact that the woman rides the beast indicates symbolically that the political and religious character of the Roman Empire work closely together with the woman in a dominant position and the beast as supporting the woman.

The traditional interpretation of this passage has identified the woman with the Roman Catholic Church. It should be observed, however, that this is a picture which is prophetically future and describes not the Roman church alone, but all Christendom combined under the Roman banner in that future day. It is most natural to assume that there would be an alliance between the Roman church, including all Christendom, and the revived Roman Empire.

The description of the woman in Revelation 17:4 is in keeping with the religious trappings of ceremonial Romanism where the purple and the scarlet color accompanied by gold, precious stones, and pearls are all too common. As this alliance of the woman with the political power constitutes spiritual fornication, she is described as guilty of this abomination.

Most significant is the title written on her forehead described as a mystery, namely, BABYLON THE GREAT, THE MOTHER OF HARLOTS AND ABOMINATIONS OF THE EARTH. The religious impact of ancient Babylon upon subsequent religions, including Romanism, is all too evident to students of the history of religion. It was in Babylon that the idolatrous worship of nature first was developed into an extensive religious system which has been traced to Nimrod and his queen Semiramis (Genesis 10:8-10). From this stemmed many of the false religions which swept the ancient world including the worship of Baal and the custom of worshiping the queen of heaven and her supposedly miraculously born son (cp. Jeremiah 7:18; 44:17-25). In ancient religions the queen of heaven and her worship is incorporated in the religions of the Greeks as Aphrodite, among the Romans as Venus, in Egypt as Isis, as Diana in Ephesus, and as Astarte in Syria.

From the standpoint of the history of Christianity, it is important to trace the influence of Babylon upon Rome especially. The cult of the woman and the child was expelled by the Medes and the Persians under Cyrus from Babylon in 539 B.C. as it was considered detrimental to the religious convictions of the Medo-Persians. The priests and priestesses of the cult, therefore, fled to Pergamos in Asia Minor where they were welcomed. Later the center of their religion was transferred by Julius Caesar to Rome in an attempt to combine their false religion with his dictatorship and introduce a religious element into his government. It was by these steps that Babylon became identified with Rome religiously and justifies the term "mystery" meaning that it should be understood in its religious rather than its historical character. With the establishment of the western branch of the Roman church in Rome, the pagan influences of the cult which originated in Babylon soon became manifested in various rites and ceremonies of the Roman Church.

That which has been historically true will reach its maximum in the future period under the revived Roman Empire. The world church of that day, almost entirely devoid of any true Christian or Biblical elements, will be the final form of apostate Christendom. As such, it will persecute any who in that day in defiance of the church follow true faith in the Lord Jesus Christ. The persecutions of Christians in the past under the power and authority of the church will be eclipsed by this future world church described as this wicked woman "drunken with the blood of the saints, and with the blood of the martyrs of Jesus."

The political power in alliance with the religious power is described in Revelation 17:8-14 in a passage which has confounded expositors, but concerning which the main elements are clear. The beast representing the political power is described as that which "was, and is not; and shall ascend out of the bottomless pit, and go into perdition" (Revelation 17:8). Later in the same verse the beast is described as "the beast that was, and is not, and yet is" [better translated, "that was, and is not, and shall be"] (Revelation 17:8). The beast is further described by the declaration of Revelation 17:9 that "The seven heads are seven mountains, on which the woman sitteth." The explanation continues in Revelation 17:10, "And there are seven kings."

Much has been written in the debate as to whether the seven mountains here describe the city of Rome often known as the city of seven hills. Many have concluded that this passage is declaring that the seat of authority for both the political and the ecclesiastical aspects of the revived Roman Empire will be the city of Rome. The passage is, however, by no means clearly a reference to the city of Rome, as the seven kings of verse 10 seem to be an exposition of what is meant by both the seven heads and the seven mountains. If the kings are the mountains and the heads, then they do not refer to the geographic situation of the city of Rome. Some nevertheless feel that the description is such that it includes both ideas.

The seven heads seem to refer to successive stages of the Roman Empire as personified in its principal rulers. In describing the seven kings in Revelation 17:10, the passage continues, "Five are fallen, and one is, and the other is not yet come; and when he cometh, he must continue a short space." This is followed by the statement in Revelation 17:11, "And the beast that was, and is not, even he is the eighth, and is of the seven, and goeth into perdition." If the eighth beast is a person heading up a political government such as the revived Roman Empire, it would naturally follow that the seven heads which precede him are also men following in chronological order and symbolizing the principal steps in the history of the ancient Roman Empire.

It has been suggested that these five heads may refer to ancient Roman rulers who had an untimely end, but who in life were worshiped as gods. Among these could be Julius Caesar, Tiberius, Caligula, Claudius, and Nero. Some have suggested that the expression "the one is" of Revelation 17:10 refers to Domitian, the last of the Caesars, and living at the time the Apostle John wrote this book. He was to be followed by a seventh who would be a forerunner to the eighth and final ruler who will appear in the period of the revived Roman Empire prior to the second advent of Christ.

In contrast to the seven kings, which seems to refer to chronological succession of rulers, are the ten kings represented by the ten horns who reign at the same time as the eighth beast. These are described as minor rulers supporting the rule of the one who is over them. In the end they fight God and perish in the final battle of Revelation 19 (Revelation 17:13, 14; 19:17-21).

In Revelation 17:15 the narrative returns to consideration of the wicked woman who is described as sitting upon many waters in Revelation 17:1 which is here interpreted as "peoples, and multitudes, and nations, and tongues." This introduces, however, the dramatic end of the world church. According to Revelation 17:16, 17, "And the ten horns which thou sawest upon the beast, these shall hate the whore, and shall make her desolate and naked, and shall eat her flesh, and burn her with fire. For God hath put in their hearts to fulfil his will, and to agree, and give their kingdom unto the beast, until the words of God shall be fulfilled." Probably at the beginning of the last three and a half years (the great tribulation preceding the second coming of Christ), the super-church which up to this time has worked with the political powers to gain control over the entire world is then suddenly destroyed. The world church has served its purpose. It has helped to place the entire world in the hands of the world political ruler. Its wealth, prestige, and organization are now at his disposal and he uses them to support his world power.

THE WORSHIP OF THE WORLD RULER

The last stage religiously of the times of the Gentiles will feature the worship of the world ruler. Concerning this, many Scriptures make a contribution. In Daniel 11:36-45 a description is given of the last days preceding the second advent of Christ. In this section described as "the time of the end" (Daniel 11:35), a king will appear who is described as an absolute monarch. Expositors have not been entirely agreed as to the particular identity of this king. Some have regarded him as a ruler in the Holy Land, possibly of Jewish background. A more likely interpretation, however, is that this king is none other than the prince that shall come of Daniel 9:26 and the same as the little horn of Daniel 7:3, who at the beginning of the great tribulation will take the role of world ruler.

The description of the king reveals him as an absolute ruler. According to Daniel 11:36, "The king shall do according to his will; and he shall exalt himself, and magnify himself above every god, and shall speak marvellous things against the God of gods, and shall prosper till the indignation be accomplished: for that that is determined shall be done." The fact that he is described as an absolute ruler and that none is greater than he would seem to identity him clearly as the world ruler. He is also described as magnifying himself above God and taking the place of God which is also an accurate description of this world ruler during the time of the great tribulation. It would therefore seem unlikely that he would be a subordinate ruler who would not be in a position of power to accomplish either absolute political government or to demand that people would recognize him as God.

Much has been written on Daniel 11:37, 38 where the statement is made concerning him, "Neither shall he regard the God of his fathers, nor the desire of women, nor regard any god: for he shall magnify himself above all. But in his estate shall he honour the God of forces: and a god whom his fathers knew not shall he honour with gold, and silver, and with precious stones, and pleasant things."

The expression that he shall not regard "the God of his fathers" has been interpreted by some as indicating a Jewish background. The characteristic Hebrew, however, for this expression in the entire Old Testament is the "Jehovah of his fathers" rather than the "Elohim of his fathers" as it is here. The term *Jehovah* is used only of the God of Israel, but the term *Elohim* is used both of the God of Israel and of heathen gods, and it also lends itself to translation as a term which is plural. The better translation is, "He shall not regard the gods of his fathers." This means that he will disregard whatever religion his forefathers followed. He also disregards "the desire of women" referring to the desire of women to be the mother of the Messiah. He puts aside the Messianic hope of a Saviour and Deliverer for Israel. Then to make it plain Daniel continues to record the message of the angel that this character will not regard any god, but shall consider himself above all deities. The world ruler who heads the revived Roman Empire will require the entire world to worship him.

In Daniel 11:38 he is described as worshiping "the God of forces." This is better understood as "the God of fortresses" or symbolically the worship of the power of military might. This indicates that this ruler, on the one hand, requires all to worship him as God, and, on the other hand, has respect only for military might. By this means he puts aside any recognition of the true God, any consideration of the supernatural sovereignty of God, and relying on satanic power attributes to himself all the prerogative of both God and supreme ruler of the entire world.

The description thus given in Daniel 11 is supported by New Testament additional revelation. According to II Thessalonians 2: 3, 4 in the future day of the Lord there will appear a lawless one or "man of sin" who will be "the son of perdition; Who opposeth and exalteth himself above all that is called God, or that is worshiped; so that he as God sitteth in the temple of God, shewing himself that he is God." This passage prophesies that the world ruler who attributes to himself the prerogatives of deity, having desecrated the temple set aside for Jewish worship under the covenant of Daniel 9:27, probably through the form of an idol will demand that people worship him. The universal worship of the world ruler is stated explicitly in Revelation 13:8, "And all that dwell upon the earth shall worship him."

THE FUTURE WORLD RELIGIOUS LEADER

The future world ruler is supported in his efforts to gain the worship of the entire world by the second beast of Revelation 13:

11-18 who originated as the supreme religious head of the world church and when this was destroyed is perpetuated in power as a supporting personage in the efforts of the beast to gain the worship of the entire world.

According to Revelation 13:11-15 he has remarkable powers attributed to Satan. He causes fire to come down from heaven and performs other miracles including an apparent ability to simulate life, or breath, in the idol of the world ruler to deceive men into thinking that the image has life. The expression in Revelation 13: 15, "And he had power to give life unto the image of the beast," is better translated, "And he hath power to give breath unto the image of the beast." The appeal to universal recognition of the beast as God, supported as he is by the second beast or the false prophet, is enforced by the edict that all shall be put to death who do not worship the image. Economic pressure is also put upon the entire world in that all receive the mark of the beast, namely, some token indicating that they are a worshiper of the beast as an identifying symbol to permit them to buy and sell.

The satanic power of this period exceeds that of any previous time and men are put in complete bondage to the worship of the beast except for those who in that day, in spite of the difficulties and even martyrdom, do come to Christ in salvation and resist the pressures to worship the world ruler. In this way the supreme power of the final world ruler and the empire which he creates is used by Satan to enslave the souls of men and bring upon the world deception of a religious character which will blind the eyes of the great majority of the world to the true facts concerning Jesus Christ.

The extreme deceptive character of this total program centering as it does in the world ruler is pictured graphically in II Thessalonians 2:8-12 where he is described as working with satanic power, deceiving those who would not receive the love of the truth. The Scriptures solemnly conclude, "And for this cause God shall send them strong delusion, that they should believe a lie: That they all might be damned who believed not the truth, but had pleasure in unrighteousness" (II Thessalonians 2:11, 12).

When the great opportunity in this present age of grace of receiving Christ as Saviour, accompanied as it is by the convicting work of the Spirit, is spurned it leads into this period during which satanic deception will reach new heights and the great mass of the world's population will blindly follow their leader to their doom. The political and spiritual warfare attributed to the beast in Daniel 7:21, 25 will have its literal fulfillment.

These great prophecies predicting the rise of the ten-nation confederacy headed by a Roman ruler who ultimately will gain control over this entire world are the major prophetic program of the period between the rapture and Christ's second coming to the earth. Into this context fit many other prophetic Scriptures such as the great battle of Ezekiel 38 and 39 and the final conflict in which the king of the south, kings of the east, and the king of the north are engaged in deadly struggle with the head of the Roman Empire at the very time that Christ returns in power and glory. Because of its strategic importance in the sequence of the events of the end time, the great battle of Ezekiel 38 and 39 will next be considered.

Chapter X

THE KING OF THE NORTH:
THE NORTHERN CONFEDERACY

In the warfare that characterizes the end of the age, the Scriptures predict a great world conflict which eventually involves all the nations of the earth. In the Scriptures that portray these stirring events, three major crises may be observed. First, a crisis in the Mediterranean area leads to the formation of the revived Roman Empire composed of a ten-nation confederacy. This is occasioned by the rise of the Roman "prince that shall come" (Daniel 9:26) who subdues three of the kings and secures the submission of the seven remaining rulers. His successful conquest of these ten kingdoms, outlined in Daniel 7:23-26, makes the Roman ruler supreme in his control of this revived form of the ancient Roman Empire.

The second phase of the struggle is recorded in Ezekiel 38 and 39. The great battle there described may be the forerunner of the expansion of the Roman Empire from domination of the Mediterranean area to the role of a world empire embracing all nations of the earth (cp. Daniel 7:23; Revelation 13:7, 8). The third phase of the world struggle is at the end of the great tribulation period just before the second coming of Christ, when major sections of the world rebel against the Roman ruler as their leader. A gigantic world war ensues with the Holy Land as its focal point (Daniel 11:40-45; Revelation 16:12-16).

Expositors are by no means agreed as to the precise details of these events or their place in the sequence. It is possible, however, to be sure about such facts as the geographic origination of military forces which converge upon the Holy Land, described as coming from the north, the east, and the south. All of these forces seem to be in opposition to the Roman ruler who may be called the king of the west, although the Scriptures never assign him this title.

The prophet Daniel in his summary of the world struggle which ends the age declares: "And at the time of the end shall the king of the south push at him: and the king of the north shall come against him like a whirlwind, with chariots, and with horsemen, and with many ships; and he shall enter into the countries, and shall overflow and pass over" (Daniel 11:40). The reference to the king of the north in this passages raises the question concerning Russia and other countries to the north of the Holy Land which figure in this final world struggle. A major contribution to this subject is found in the prophecies of Ezekiel concerning a great invastion of the Holy Land from the north in the end time.

THE RISE OF RUSSIA IN THE TWENTIETH CENTURY

One of the significant aspects of modern life which all have observed in the last quarter of a century is the remarkable rise of Russia to a place of world prominence. At the close of World War II, Russia as a nation was crushed, its manpower destroyed, its cities in ruin. It was a nation that would have been utterly defeated if it had not been for American help. Since World War II, Russia has recovered and has become a prominent nation with world-wide influence which few nations have ever achieved. Today, Russia is one of the principal competitors of the United States of America for world fame and world leadership. Through the instrument of communism and nations which share Russia's convictions on communism, almost half of the world's population is in some sense or other in the Russian orbit. Such a phenomenal rise of a nation so godless and blasphemous must have some prophetic significance.

DOES THE BIBLE CONTAIN PROPHECY ABOUT RUSSIA?

In the study of prophecy, care must be taken not to create doctrine without proper Scriptural support. Many aspects of prophecy in the Bible may be understood only partially. There are great themes of prophecy, however, which do not rest on isolated texts, but upon extended portions of the Word of God. As these Scriptures are studied, some settled conclusions can be reached regarding the main movements of God in the prophetic future.

The word *Russia* is not found in the English Bible, and at first glance it would seem that there is nothing in the Bible that would give any information about Russia. A more careful investigation, however, reveals that there are two long chapters in the Bible which seem to concern themselves with the nation Russia, with certain other portions of Scripture which cast added light upon the subject. Not only has the Bible something to say about Russia, but what it reveals is of tremendous significance in God's prophetic program.

In Ezekiel 38 and 39, a description is given of a war between Israel and a nation which many have identified as Russia. The two chapters mentioned describe the invasion of the land of Israel by the armies of Russia and the nations that are associated with her. The Scriptures are plain that this is a military invasion and reveal many details about the situation existing at the time of that invasion. The dramatic outcome of the battle is the utter destruction of the army that invades the land of Israel. Written by the prophet Ezekiel, who himself was in exile from the land of Israel, this prophecy was inspired by the Spirit of God. A natural question can be raised, however, inasmuch as this was written some twenty-five hundred years ago, whether this passage has already been fulfilled.

The land of Israel has been the scene of many wars, and invasions have come from various parts of the world, north, east, and south. Many times the march of soldier's feet has been heard crossing the little nation of Israel. The Bible records some of these wars and some of them have occurred since the canon of Scripture was closed. It would be difficult to examine the details of all these wars; however, if one did, he would find that none of them correspond to this prophecy. There never has been a war with Israel which fulfills the prophecies of Ezekiel 38 and 39. If one believes that the Bible is the Word of God and that it is infallible and must be fulfilled, the only logical conclusion is that this portion of Scripture, like many others, is still due a future fulfillment.

THE IDENTIFICATION OF RUSSIA

In beginning the study of this chapter, it is necessary to establish beyond any question that this passage deals with the nation Russia, inasmuch as the term itself does not occur. There are a number of important factors which lead to the conclusion that the only nation which could possibly fulfill the specifications of these two chapters is the nation Russia. In the study of this chapter the American Standard Version will be used because of its clarification of certain difficult passages.

First of all, it is important to note the geographic description which is given. The terms "king of the north" and "king of the south" were used in Daniel 11:5-35 to describe the rulers to the north and south of Palestine who engaged in constant warfare in the second and third centuries B.C. This is now fulfilled prophecy. The king of the north and king of the south of Daniel 11:40-45, however, are future rulers involved in warfare in the end time. This is still unfulfilled prophecy. Ezekiel 38 and 39 fit into this future picture.

According to Ezekiel, the invading armies come to the land of Israel from "the uttermost part of the north" or as we would put it from the far north. In the Authorized Version the expression is translated merely "from the north," but in the more literal translation of the Hebrew found in the American Standard Version it is rendered, "the uttermost parts of the north," i.e., the extreme north. The important point is that it designates not merely the direction from which the army attacks Israel, but specifies the geographic origination of the army from a territory located in the far north. The house of Togarmah, one of the nations that is associated with Russia in this invasion, also comes from "the uttermost parts of the north" (Ezekiel 38:6).

A similar statement concerning the invader is made in verse 15, "Thou shalt come from thy place out of the uttermost parts of the north, thou, and many peoples with thee, all of them riding upon horses, a great company and a mighty army" (ASV). Again in Ezekiel 39:2, God says to them, "I will turn thee about, and will lead thee on, and will cause thee to come up from the uttermost parts of the north; and I will bring thee upon the mountains of Israel" (ASV). Three times in these chapters this army is stated to come from the extreme north.

If one takes any map of the world and draws a line north of the land of Israel he will inevitably come to the nation Russia. As soon as the line is drawn to the far north beyond Asia Minor and the Black Sea it is in Russia and continues to be in Russia for many hundreds of miles all the way to the Arctic Circle. Russia today spreads east and west some 6,000 miles, and one cannot escape Russia if he goes north of the Holy Land. On the basis of geography alone, it seems quite clear that the only nation which could possibly be referred to as coming from the far north would be the nation Russia. The suggestion that the nation is ancient Assyria revived is rendered improbable by the geographic description.

As the Scriptures are further examined, not only geographic data but also some confirming linguistic evidence is discovered. In the opening portion of Ezekiel 38, in verses 1 through 6, some names are mentioned which identify the invaders. This portion indicates that the Word of the Lord came to Ezekiel saying,

> Son of man, set thy face toward Gog, of the land of Magog, the prince of Rosh, Meshech, and Tubal, and prophesy against him, and say, Thus saith the Lord Jehovah: Behold, I am against thee, O Gog, prince of Rosh, Meshech, and Tubal: and I will turn thee about, and put hooks into thy jaws, and I will bring thee forth, and all thine army, horses and horsemen, all of them clothed in full armor, a great company with buckler and shield, all of them handling swords: Persia, Cush and Put with them, all of them with shield and helmet; Gomer, and all his hordes; the house of Togarmah in the uttermost parts of the north, and all his hordes; even many peoples with thee (ASV).

Most of the terms in this portion of Scripture are quite strange to us and do not immediately connote anything relating to Russia. Certain facts are discovered as the passage is examined more particularly. This portion of Scripture is a message from God delivered by the prophet Ezekiel, directed to a person whose name is Gog, who is described as of the land of Magog and apparently the ruler of this land. The term "Magog" is mentioned in Genesis 10:2. There we learn that Magog was the second son of Japheth, the son of Noah.

Magog is best identified with the Scythians, a people descended from Magog. The ancient historian Josephus makes that identification and we have no reason to question it. The Scythians apparently lived immediately to the north of what was later to be the land of Israel, then some of them emigrated north, going all the way to the Arctic Circle. In other words, their posterity was scattered precisely over the geographical area that today is called Russia.

In Ezekiel 38 Gog is described as "the prince of Rosh" (ASV). The Authorized Version expresses it as the "chief prince." The translation, "the prince of Rosh," is a more literal rendering of the Hebrew. "Rosh" may be the root of the modern term, Russia. In the study of how ancient words come into modern language, it is quite common for the consonants to remain the same and the vowels to be changed. In the word "Rosh," if the vowel "o" is changed to "u" it becomes the root of the modern word, Russia, with the suffix added. In other words, the word itself seems to be an early form of the word from which the modern word, Russia, comes. Genesius, the famous lexicographer, gives the assurance that this is a proper identification, that is, that Rosh is an early form of the word from which we get Russia.

The two terms, "Meshech" and "Tubal," also correspond to some prominent words in Russia. The term "Meshech" is similar to the modern name Moscow, and "Tubal," obviously, is similar to the name of one of the prominent Asiatic provinces of Russia, the province of Tobolsk. When this evidence is put together, it points to the conclusion that these terms are early references to portions of Russia, and therefore, the geographic argument is reinforced by the linguistic argument and supports the idea that this invading force comes from Russia.

As the prophecy is examined further it becomes obvious that the invaders utterly disregard God, because any nation that attacks the nation of Israel by so much is disregarding the Word of God. The godlessness of the invading army attacking Israel also points the finger to the nation Russia. On the basis of these three arguments, the geographic argument, the linguistic argument, and what might be called the theological argument, it may be concluded that the reference is to the nation Russia. In fact, there is no other reasonable alternative. Russia is today the only nation which seems to fit the picture.

A number of nations are associated with Russia in the invasion, but not too much is known about them. Persia, of course, is in that general area. Cush is another name for Ethiopia, which poses a problem because today Ethiopia is to the south. The term *Cush* may have been applied to other geographic areas, including that to the north of the land of Israel. The term, "Put," is a difficult expression about which little is known. In verse 6 the term, "Gomer," is identified by most as referring to the ancient Cimmerians, a portion of whom lived in what today is called southern or western Germany. Togarmah is commonly recognized as referring to the Armenians, who at one time lived immediately north of the land of Israel, and they, too, to some extent emigrated to the north. The nations which accompany Russia, for the most part, fit properly into the picture of assisting Russia in this invasion of the land of Israel.

The Predicted Invasion of Israel

The actual invasion is described in Ezekiel 38:8-12. Some of the distinctive facts mentioned about the particular situation which will exist when this war begins are of utmost significance in the light of the world situation today. In this passage the "thou" refers throughout to Russia or to Gog. The term "they" is used to refer to Israel. Beginning in verse 8 and continuing through verse 16, the passage reads as follows:

> After many days thou shalt be visited: in the latter years thou shalt come into the land that is brought back from the sword, that is gathered out of many peoples, upon the mountains of Israel, which have been a continual waste; but it is brought forth out of the peoples, and they shall dwell securely, all of them. And thou shalt ascend, thou shalt come like a storm, thou shalt be like a cloud to cover the land, thou, and all thy hordes, and many peoples with thee.
>
> Thus saith the Lord Jehovah: It shall come to pass in that day, that things shall come into thy mind, and thou shalt devise an evil device: and thou shalt say, I will go up to the land of unwalled villages; I will go to them that are at rest, that dwell securely, all of them dwelling without walls, and having neither bars nor gates; to take the spoil and to take the prey; to turn thy hand against the waste places that are now inhabited, and against the people that are gathered out of the nations, that have gotten cattle and goods, that dwell in the middle of the earth. Sheba, and Dedan, and the merchants of Tarshish, with all the young lions thereof, shall say unto thee, Art thou come to take the spoil? hast thou assembled thy company to take the prey? to carry away silver and gold, to take away cattle and goods, to take great spoil?
>
> Therefore, son of man, prophesy, and say unto Gog, Thus saith the Lord Jehovah: In that day when my people Israel dwelleth securely, shalt thou not know it? And thou shalt come from thy place out of the uttermost parts of the north, thou, and many peoples with thee, all of them riding upon horses, a great company and a mighty army; and thou shalt come up against my people Israel, as a cloud to cover the land: it shall come to pass in the latter days, that I will bring thee against my land, that the nations may know me, when I shall be sanctified in thee, O Gog, before their eyes (asv).

Invasion After Israel's Regathering

Some highly significant facts are given in the above passage concerning the precise situation existing when the invasion takes place. There are a number of references to the fact that the people of Israel are back in their ancient land. This of course is of tremendous importance because it is only in our generation that the people of Israel have gone back to their ancient land. In A.D. 70, Titus, the Roman general, conquered Jerusalem, utterly destroyed it, and killed up to a million of the Jews. Roman soldiers later systematically went throughout the entire land of Israel destroying every building, sawing down or uprooting every tree, and doing everything they could to make the land totally uninhabitable. The result was that the land of Israel lay in waste for several generations. The children of Israel from that day to this have been scattered over the face of the earth.

At the close of World War II the children of Israel began to return to their ancient land in large numbers. Some had gone earlier, but they were few in number. They built up their strength and numbers until finally they were recognized as a nation in May, 1948. At that time one million Jews were back in their ancient land, the largest return since the days of the Exodus. In the years since, their number has doubled, and today there are two million Israelites under their own flag, speaking the Hebrew language, and reviving and restoring their ancient land to a scene of fertility, wealth, and prosperity. These facts are tremendously significant, for the return of Israel has occurred in our generation.

Ezekiel's prophecy obviously could not have been fulfilled prior to 1945, for the nation Israel was not regathered to their ancient land. Until our generation, Israel's situation did not correspond to that which is described in Ezekiel's passage. Ezekiel's prophecy of twenty-five hundred years ago seems to have anticipated the return of Israel to their ancient land as a prelude to the climax of this present age.

INVASION AFTER REBUILDING OF CITIES

Another important aspect of the prophecy is found in verse eleven where it states that the people of Israel will be dwelling "securely, all of them dwelling without walls, and having neither bars nor gates." It was customary in ancient times, whenever a city prospered, to build a wall around it. One can go to ancient lands and see the ruins of walls around most important cities. They would, at least, have a fortress with a wall around it to which they could retire if the houses themselves were scattered and a wall about the houses was impracticable. In other words, it was customary to build walls about cities. In our modern day, this custom has been discontinued for the obvious reason that a wall is no protection against modern warfare.

If one goes to Israel today, though one can see many fabulous cities being built and marvelous developments taking place, one will not find a single new city with a wall built around it. They are cities without walls. How did Ezekiel know that at a future time the war situation would be such that cities would be built without walls? Of course, the answer is a simple one. He was guided by the inspiration of God, and it was not a matter of his own wisdom. But in this scene he is describing a modern situation, something that could not and would not be true back in the days of old, before Christ. This detail is very important because unwalled villages point to Israel's situation today.

INVASION AT A TIME OF ISRAEL'S PROSPERITY

A third feature may also be observed. This portion of Scripture is explicit that one of the reasons why Russia wants to conquer the land of Israel is that it had become a land of great wealth. Russia comes to take a prey, to take silver and gold, and the wealth that has been accumulated (cp. Ezekiel 38:12, 13). Until our generation, the geographic area of the land of Israel was anything but something to be prized. It did not have any wealth; it was a land that was strewn with stones; a land that was backward as far as civilization is concerned. Many of the areas that at one time were fruitful in Bible times were unused prior to Israel's reclamation. The land was eroded and useless as far as agriculture is concerned.

Since the Israelites have gone back to their ancient land, they have done fabulous things. They have taken rocky fields, gathered the stones in piles along the edge, and cultivated and irrigated the ground and made it to bring forth abundantly. They have reclaimed swamps where mosquitoes and malaria made civilization impossible before. In fact, the first people that tried to do something about it lost their lives because of the unhealthy situation. These former swamps are today one of the richest areas of farm land in the entire world. It is almost incredible what has occurred there since 1948. They have spent money, they have put forth extreme effort, and from one end of Israel to the other tremendous progress is in evidence. The result is today that Israel is beginning once again to be a nation that has wealth. A great deal is being exported to other countries, and money is beginning to flow back to the little nation of Israel.

In addition to agricultural wealth, there are some factors that Ezekiel did not know which we know today. One factor is that to the east of the land of Israel are tremendous oil reserves. One of the largest and richest oil fields in the entire world is in the Middle East. It is outside the present geographic area of Israel, but the nation that wants to control that oil land must control the nation Israel. It is obvious that the tremendous oil reserves of the Middle East are one of the prizes that Russia wants to secure.

Another aspect of wealth which has come to light in modern times is the chemical value of the Dead Sea area, where water has evaporated for centuries, leaving its mineral deposit. Israel has established a plant at the south end of the Dead Sea and is reclaiming the chemicals. Millions of dollars of those chemicals are being shipped, and they have just begun to tap this wealth. Ezekiel anticipated the time when the land of Israel would be fabulously wealthy.

Military Importance of Israel

In addition to all these factors, it is obvious that the geographic location of the Middle East, being as it is a hub between three major continents — Europe, Asia, and Africa — is of tremendous strategic importance to any nation that wants to dominate the world. The geographic significance of the Middle East alone would be worth a real effort on the part of Russia to have this portion of the world under its control. Again Ezekiel anticipates today's situation.

The Destruction of the Invading Army

When the Russian army comes down upon this land they are met with complete and utter destruction. Strange to say, as we examine the Scriptures, we do not find them being destroyed by an opposing army, but rather it seems to be by divine intervention. Somehow God by His own power destroys the army. In Ezekiel 38:19, 20 a description is given of earthquakes, mountains falling, and other disturbances which hinder their progress.

Then God declares:

> And I will call for a sword against him unto all my mountains, saith the Lord Jehovah: every man's sword shall be against his brother. And with pestilence and with blood will I enter into judgment with him; and I will rain upon him, and upon his hordes, and upon the many

peoples that are with him, an overflowing shower, and great hailstones, fire, and brimstone. And I will magnify myself, and sanctify myself, and I will make myself known in the eyes of many nations; and they shall know that I am Jehovah (Ezekiel 38:21-23, ASV).

The army's destruction is portrayed in Ezekiel 39:4 ff. God declares: "Thou shalt fall upon the mountains of Israel, thou, and all thy hordes, and the peoples that are with thee: I will give thee unto the ravenous birds of every sort, and to the beasts of the field to be devoured." In other words, the army is completely destroyed, and the means used are earthquakes, hailstones, fire and brimstone. It seems also that parts of the army begin to fight each other, so that every man's sword is against his brother.

Some natural questions are raised about this. Some have suggested that the description of hailstones, fire and brimstone might be Ezekiel's way of describing modern warfare, such as atomic warfare. There is a possibility that Ezekiel was using terms that he knew to describe a future situation for which he did not have a vocabulary. The language of Scripture indicates, however, that the victory over this invading horde is something that God does. It is God, Himself, who is destroying the army.

In any case, regardless of the means, the army is completely destroyed and chapter 39 goes on to describe the aftermath. For months thereafter they have the awful task of burying the dead. For a long period after that men are given full-time employment as additional bodies are discovered, and the process of burial continues. Attention is also directed to the debris of the battle. It is used as kindling wood for some seven years. The general character of this battle and its outcome seems to be quite clear, even though we may have some questions and problems about the details.

TIME OF THE INVASION

One of the principal questions one could ask about this battle is, When is the battle going to occur? It has not occurred in the past. What indication do we have in this portion of Scripture that the battle will occur at a specific time? Unfortunately, varying opinions have been offered by capable Bible scholars on this point, and there has been considerable disagreement. Some have felt that the battle will take place before the rapture, others believe it will take place in connection with the battle of Armageddon, or the battle of the Great Day of God Almighty, at the end of the great tribulation. Some place it at the beginning of the millennium, as an act of rebellion against Christ. Some find it at the end of the millennium, for there is a reference to Gog and Magog in Revelation 20. Others put it in the earlier part of Daniel's seventieth week, just before the great tribulation.

It will not be possible to consider all these views in detail, but there are some hints that provide a good clue as to when this battle will take place. One of the hints given is that the battle takes place at a time when Israel has been regathered into their ancient land, and are dwelling securely and at rest. There are not too many times when Israel is at rest in God's prophetic program. They have been scattered and persecuted over the face of the earth, and not even in the future will Israel have many periods of rest.

Certainly Israel is not at rest today. Israel is an armed camp, living under a truce with their Arab neighbors about them. Their enemies would drive every Israelite into the Mediterranean Sea and kill them if they could. The reason that they do not is because, humanly speaking, Israel has a good army which is more than a match for its neighbors. Today an armed truce and a no-man's land separate Israel from their enemy.

Every young Israeli man is required to have two and one-half years of military training and every young woman two years of military training. While the women are trained for jobs that are not necessarily of combatant type, they also learn to use weapons, so that if they need to fight, they can. After military training, many of them are settled in villages near the border, where they can serve a double purpose — following their occupation, whatever it is, and serving as guards for the border of Israel. Israel's state of unrest does not correspond to Ezekiel's prophecy. If Russia should invade the Middle East today, it would not be a fulfillment of this portion of Scripture. That has to take place when Israel is at rest.

One point at which Israel will be at rest is in the millennial kingdom. But we are told expressly that, in the millennial kingdom, there will be no war (Isaiah 2:4), and only when the rebellion occurs at the end of the millennium when Satan is let loose (Revelation 20:7-9) does war break out. Certainly Israel is not going to be at rest under these circumstances either, once Satan is let loose.

Some have suggested that Israel will be at rest in the period of great triblulation, and that the prophecy of Russia will be fulfilled at that time. In the time of great tribulation, Israel will not be at rest, for Christ told them to flee to the mountains to escape their persecutors. Therefore the invasion described by Ezekiel could not be a part of the battle of Armageddon, or the battle of the Great Day of God Almighty.

There is only one period in the future that clearly fits this description of Ezekiel, and that is the first half of Daniel's seventieth week of God's program for Israel (Daniel 9:27). After the church has been raptured and saints have been raised from the dead and the living saints have been caught up to be with the Lord, a confederacy of nations will emerge in the Mediterranean Sea. Out of that confederacy will come a strong man who will become its dictator (discussed in previous chapters). He is described in Daniel 9:26 as "the prince that shall come." He will enter into a seven-year covenant of protection and peace with the people of Israel (Daniel 9:27).

Under that covenant, Israel will be able to relax, for their Gentile enemies will have become their friends, apparently guaranteed their borders and promised them freedom. During that first three and one-half years, we have the one time when regathered Israel is at rest and secure. Apparently Russia will invade the land of Israel during that period, possibly toward its close, and the Scripture will then be fulfilled.

Problems of Interpretation

There are some other problems in the passage which merit study. A reference is made to bows and arrows, to shields and chariots, and to swords. These, of course, are antiquated weapons from the standpoint of modern warfare. The large use of horses is understandable as Russia today uses horses a great deal in connection with their army. But why should they use armor, spears, bows and arrows? This certainly poses a problem.

There have been two or more answers given. One of them is this that Ezekiel is using language with which he was familiar — the weapons that were common in his day — to anticipate modern weapons. What he is saying is that when this army comes, it will be fully equipped with the weapons of war. Such an interpretation, too, has problems. We are told in the passage that they used the wooden shafts of the spears and the bow and arrows for kindling wood. If these are symbols, it would be difficult to burn symbols. However, even in modern warfare there is a good deal of wood used. Possibly this is the explanation. We are not in a position today to settle this problem with any finality.

A second solution is that the battle is preceded by a disarmament agreement between nations. If this were the case, it would be necessary to resort to primitive weapons easily and secretly made if a surprise attack were to be achieved. This would allow a literal interpretation of the passage.

A third solution has also been suggested based on the premise that modern missile warfare will have developed in that day to the point where missiles will seek out any considerable amount of metal. Under these circumstances, it would be necessary to abandon the large use of metal weapons and substitute wood such as is indicated in the primitive weapons. Whatever the explanation, the most sensible interpretation is that the passage refers to actual weapons pressed into use because of the peculiar circumstances of that day.

THE FUTURE OF RUSSIA

The general character of the passage, the nature of the war, the invasion when it comes, and the outcome is, however, perfectly clear. What significance does it have to the modern scene? First of all, if we understand the passage correctly, Russia, instead of being a nation which is going to dominate the whole world, is headed for a tremendous military defeat. It is not possible to predict what is going to happen between now and the time this battle takes place, but the Bible seems quite clear that there is no room for a Russian-dominated world empire. The Bible prophesies only four world empires. The empire of the great tribulation period which will come as a form of the revived Roman Empire, is the final form of the fourth empire of Daniel, not a Russian Empire. This, in turn, will be succeeded by the millennial reign of Christ.

The passage seems to confirm that Russia, instead of becoming a world power that is going to dominate the whole world, is instead headed for an awful defeat, a judgment from God because of its blasphemy and ungodliness. If this becomes true during the time of the seventieth week of Daniel, it may explain something that otherwise might be difficult.

THE EMERGENCE OF A WORLD EMPIRE

We know that in the last half of Daniel's seventieth week there will be a world government headed by the ruler of the Mediterranean confederacy. The question is, how does he forge this world empire so quickly and so easily, and apparently without fighting for it? We learn in Revelation 13:4 that the question is asked, "Who is able to make war with him?" i.e., with the Beast. The answer is that nobody is able to make war with him. It should be obvious that if Russia and her satellites are destroyed as military powers, the other side of the balance of power, represented by the Mediterranean confederacy, is then in a position to dominate the whole world. Nobody is able, for at least a time, to contest their right to rule.

The destruction of the Russian army may be the preface to the world government which will sweep the world during the last half of Daniel's seventieth week and be in power at the time Christ comes back to establish His millennial kingdom. These two portions of Scripture, while they concern themselves with a future war, are of tremendous significance as we face the present world scene and the dominance of Russia as a military power. We can trust that God, in due time, and perhaps sooner than we think, will bring these Scriptures to their sure conclusion and fulfillment.

THE EMERGENCE OF A WORLD RELIGION

There is another aspect of the problem that is worthy of careful consideration. What is the relation of all this to what we today call communism? It must be recognized that communism and Russia are not synonymous, for there are nations which are communistic which are not necessarily following Russia's leadership. Communism is a form of political philosophy; it is a form of religion. It is an ideology which is not limited to the Russian nation even though Russia has provided the major spark for it.

Communism is an atheistic religion — a religion denying that God exists, a religion denying that there is anything that is supernatural, a religion that recognizes only material force. If these facts are kept in mind, it becomes a most significant fact that in the false religion which will sweep the world during the time of the great tribulation there are precisely the same elements present.

The false religion at the tribulation time is described in Daniel 11:36-38. This portion of Scripture describes the king who shall do according to his will, i.e., an absolute ruler. The king is believed by many to be the future world ruler of which the Scriptures speak, as indicated in previous discussion. He may be "the prince that shall come" of Daniel 9:26. In Daniel 11:37, it states of this ruler, "Neither shall he regard the gods of his fathers, nor the desire of women, nor regard any god; for he shall magnify himself above all" (ASV). In other words, this ruler will push aside any previous kind of religion, any god which had been previously worshiped, and in their place he will put himself as the object of universal worship.

In explanation of this, it states in Daniel 11:38, "But in his place shall he honor the god of fortresses" (ASV). In the Authorized Version it is translated, "the god of forces," but the word "forces" represents military forces. It is a recognition of the power to make war. This Scripture reveals, in a word, that the only deity this man will recognize and respect is the power to make war. He is an absolute atheist, an absolute materialist.

It should be clear that the rapid rise of communism in our generation has swept within its folds almost half of the world's population, a phenomenon without parallel in the history of the world. While the ultimate false religion will not be communism in the form we know it today, communism may very well be the forerunner and preparation for the future world religion that will sweep all the world during the time of the great tribulation.

Millions of young people today are being systematically taught atheism, denying that any God exists. They are taught to give their complete allegiance to their political leaders, and to die, if need be, for the cause that this represents. Certainly, as they are being conditioned, brainwashed, trained to think this way, the ground is being prepared for the future atheistic, blasphemous worship of Satan's man — Satan's substitute for Christ who alone has the right to rule as King of kings and Lord of lords.

In the rise of communism, something different from the rise of Russia can be seen. While the Scriptures seem to indicate that Russia as a political power will go down, the philosophy and the godlessness and the atheism which it has spawned in our modern day seem to be just the beginning of that which some day will sweep the entire world.

Those who have put their trust in the Lord Jesus can certainly have a wonderful refuge in the Word of God in facing these facts. We believe that the Lord Jesus Christ is coming first to take His body, the church, out of the world in the translation of the living and resurrection of the dead in Christ before these things come to their consummation, before Russia attacks the land of Israel, before this godless religion sweeps the world. But the very fact that these forces are in the world today, Russia, a great nation, poised to the north of the Holy Land, Israel in its place, already a nation of wealth and significance and a prize to be sought, indicates that the end may be near. Ezekiel described the building of cities without walls and anticipates a time when Israel would be secure and at rest. We see today the remarkable preparation for events which will take place after the rapture of the church. God is setting the stage in Israel, in Russia, and in communism for world events that will end the age.

We certainly must realize that this situation is not going to remain static, that it is rapidly moving to a consummation. In that consummation we believe the first important event will be Christ's coming for His own. If there ever was a generation of Bible-believing Christians who had a right to look forward to the coming of the Lord momentarily day by day, on the basis of what they see in the world, it is our present generation. Even unbelievers are telling us today that things cannot go on as they are much longer.

An interesting commentary on the widespread expectation of a coming world climax is found in the present tension between Israel and the Arab world. The efforts of Israel to secure a peace have been unavailing because of fanatical opposition on the part of the Arab world to any sort of a settlement with Israel. Any Arab ruler who would attempt to negotiate with Israel would be in danger of assassination even as one king of Jordan has already been killed. Jewish leaders, however, are still longing for the day when peace can be consummated. One of their leaders made the statement in the hearing of the writer to this effect, "Sooner or later there will rise someone who will make a covenant with the people of Israel, and as soon as he does it, while he may be very unpopular before he does it, he will be hailed as a hero and as a leader in the Middle East."

In Daniel 9:26 there is the prophecy of "the prince that shall come" who will make a covenant with Israel. We cannot presume that the covenant Israel hopes for today is necessarily Daniel's covenant, but it might be. When this Israeli leader was asked when this might come about, he replied, "It could be any day." This coming from the lips of one who is not of the Christian faith and who does not know the prophetic Scriptures was certainly almost prophetic in its character. The hour of the Lord's return may indeed be very, very near.

The rise of Russia and the widespread power and influence of communism are two important factors pointing to the conclusion that the stage is being set for the end of the age. The future invasion from the north obviously fits into our contemporary scene and adds its important evidence that time is running out and that the nations will soon move into their final crisis.

The invasion pictured in Ezekiel 38 and 39 is probably, however, not the last invasion of the king of the north. As previously indicated in Daniel 11, there is evidence that the king of the north will again come upon the Holy Land. According to Daniel 11:40 a series of actions will take part in the great battle and world struggle which will be under way at the very time that the Lord Jesus Christ returns in power and glory. As this event takes place several years after the debacle of Ezekiel 38 and 39, it appears that the king of the north is able by that time to put another army in the field and again becomes a factor in the struggle with the Roman ruler. Details of the second invasion are not given, however, except the mention in Daniel 11 and intimations that an army comes from the north in the very last days of the age.

CHAPTER XI

EGYPT AND THE KING OF THE SOUTH

For more than three thousand years before the birth of Christ, Egypt was one of the greatest civilizations of the ancient world. Although much of its history was shrouded in mystery until the last century, the careful research of archaeologists has now provided almost limitless material for Egyptology, the science of the history and culture of this great nation of the past. Both from the standpoint of world history as well as the Biblical point of view, no other nation in Africa has had such an impact upon the world as a whole. Long before Babylon became great or Greek civilization came into flower, Egypt was already a great nation with a culture, history, and literature of its own. Nourished by the rich Nile valley, a delta a dozen miles wide and extending more than 500 miles in length, the land of Egypt early became one of the important factors in Biblical history and a great political power in the Mediterranean scene.

First mention of Egypt is under its ancient name of Mizraim, one of the sons of Ham in Genesis 10:6. The name itself is in a dual number which some believe refers to the natural division of the country into upper and lower Egypt. The modern name Egypt is thought to have been derived from a king by the name of Egyptus who reigned in 1485 B.C. However, this conclusion is challenged. The Egyptians themselves referred to their land as Kemet which has the meaning, "the black land." In the Bible it is also referred to as "the land of Ham" referring to the Hamitic origin of the Egyptians.

First mention of Egypt in the history of the Old Testament occurs in Genesis 12 where it is recorded that Abraham, because of the famine in the land of Canaan, went to Egypt (Genesis 12:10). There he attempted to hide the fact that Sarah was his wife and called her his sister — a partial truth. Only by intervention of God who plagued Pharaoh was Sarah rescued from the possibility of being taken as a wife of Pharaoh, and Abraham and his wife were sent out of Egypt.

The subsequent fruit of this ill-fated venture into Egypt was that he brought Hagar back with him. She ultimately became the mother of Ishmael (Genesis 16:1-6) who became the progenitor of the Arabian tribes who caused Israel so much trouble in the years that followed. Isaac was forbidden to go down into the land of Egypt as Abraham had done (Genesis 26:2), but Ishmael guided by his mother took a wife from Egypt (Genesis 21:21). It was not until the time of Joseph that the children of Israel again entered the land of Egypt.

ISRAEL'S SOJOURN IN EGYPT

The first prophecy concerning Egypt in Scripture is found in the important fifteenth chapter of Genesis where God confirms His covenant with Abraham. This chapter becomes the cornerstone of fulfillment of the Abrahamic covenant as it relates to possession of the land ultimately to be possessed by Israel, defined as the area "from the river of Egypt unto the great river, the river Euphrates" (Genesis 15:18). The expression "the river of Egypt" is probably a reference to the small river which is the boundary between Egypt and Palestine known as Wady-el-Arish. Apart from its reference to Egypt the chapter is important for its vision of God as "a burning lamp" which some have taken as the first instance of the Shekinah glory, and for its enumeration of the important nations adjacent to Israel or occupying its land in ancient times. Ten nations are named in Genesis 15:19-21.

Of major importance in relation to prophecy relating to Egypt, however, is the statement made to Abraham in Genesis 15:13, 14: "Know of a surety that thy seed shall be a stranger in a land that is not their's, and shall serve them; and they shall afflict them four hundred years; And also that nation, whom they shall serve, will I judge: and afterward shall they come out with great substance." Although Egypt is not named, it is inescapable that this is the reference intended by the term "land that is not theirs." Thus long before the children of Israel went down into Egypt, it was predicted that they would sojourn there and be afflicted for 400 years.

Considerable attention has been given to the question of the 400 years as historical data does not necessarily support this idea.

If Israel left Egypt at the time of the Exodus about 1440 B.C. as most conservative scholars have agreed, they actually were in Egypt approximately 210 years. How can this be explained?

On the basis of the chronology of Galatians 3:17 where it is stated that the law came 430 years after the promise, a reasonable chronology is provided by beginning the 430 years at the time that Abraham left Ur of Chaldees. From that point to the birth of Isaac was a period of approximately 30 years. From the birth of Isaac to the birth of Jacob was another 60 years. From the birth of Jacob until Jacob went down into Egypt was another 130 years. This computation provides at least one good explanation for this reference to 400 years in Genesis 15. This is confirmed by the Septuagint rendering of Exodus 12:40, 41 where the children of Israel are said to have sojourned in the land of Egypt and in the land of Canaan for 430 years. This early reference to the children of Israel sojourning in the land of Egypt is one of the important milestones in prophecy in the Old Testament.

The story of how Jacob and his family went to Egypt is given in detail in Genesis, chapter 37 to chapter 50. The story's importance in the history of Israel is demonstrated in the fact that Genesis, which devotes only two chapters to the whole creation narrative and only one chapter to the entrance of sin into the human race, uses fourteen chapters to trace the history of Israel from the time of Joseph being sold as a slave until the time of his death. Egypt was to be the matrix in which Israel would grow from a family of 70 to a great nation of several million.

THE EXODUS FROM EGYPT

The history of Israel and of Egypt makes clear that the affliction or servitude mentioned in Genesis 15:13 was not always severe. However, during the latter portion of their sojourn in Egypt, there was a change in dynasty of the "Shepherd Kings" known as the Hyksos who dominated the scene for two hundred years, 1750-1570 B.C., and were in power at the time that Joseph came to Egypt. Their expulsion and the formation of the new empire beginning with Dynasty XVIII set the stage not only for Israel's period of great glory and the construction of vast buildings, but also the slavery of the people of Israel. Thutmose III, who reigned 1482-1450 B.C., conquered all of Palestine, and defeated the Hittites. Thutmose III was followed by Amenhotep II (1450-1425 B.C.), the Pharaoh with whom the children of Israel had to deal in connection with the Exodus. The subsequent decline of Egypt and her loosening grip on Palestine ultimately made possible the conquest of the land by the children of Israel without Egyptian interference.

Contributing to the confusion which arose in the reign of Amenhotep II were the series of plagues inflicted upon the Egyptians recorded in the early chapters of Exodus. The story of Israel's deliverance from Egypt and the destruction of the Egyptian host in the Red Sea marks the close of the Egyptian bondage and the beginning of Israel as a separate nation.

The subsequent history of Egypt included constant contact with the children of Israel. The large part that Egypt played in the Old Testament is borne out by more than 700 references to Egypt in the Old Testament contrasted to less than 30 in the New Testament. Most of these are reminders to Israel that they were "brought up out of the land of Egypt" and this recurring phrase occurs approximately 125 times.

Commercial relationships with Egypt reached a high point during the reign of Solomon. According to I Kings 3:1, "Solomon made affinity with Pharaoh king of Egypt, and took Pharaoh's daughter, and brought her into the city of David." I Kings 10:28 records that Egypt was the source of the horses Solomon used in his host of chariots for which he was famous. Solomon had 12,000 horsemen and 1400 chariots with both the horses and the chariots purchased out of Egypt (I Kings 10:26, 29). Other commodities such as linen yarn were bought in Egypt. The commercial alliance with Egypt and Solomon's host of horses and chariots were in violation of the Word of God (Deuteronomy 17:16) and were a part of the secularization in Solomon's reign which led to Israel's spiritual downfall after his death.

Along with Assyria and Babylon, Egypt was one of the great nations of the past and is destined to have its important place in prophetic fulfillment at the end of the age. Egypt, however, was not the benefactor, but traditionally the enemy of Israel. This is seen in the sad commentary which forms a footnote to Solomon's relationships to Egypt recorded in the reign of Rehoboam, his successor, when Shishak king of Egypt conquered Jerusalem in the fifth year of the reign of Rehoboam and took away all of the treasures of the king's house and of the house of the Lord (I Kings 14: 25, 26). Egypt, under the able leadership of the Egyptian ruler

Pharaoh-Necho (609-593 b.c.), once again conquered Palestine during the reign of King Josiah (631-608 b.c.). The Egyptian bondage, however, was soon to end and be replaced by the Babylonian captivity with the rise of Nebuchadnezzar and the conquering of Jerusalem in 606 b.c. Jeremiah the prophet of the exile was carried against his will to Egypt where he died. The Old Testament history does not record anything further of importance concerning Egypt.

Where Biblical history stops, however, the prophetic narrative begins. Egypt was destined to have an important place in subsequent history as related to Israel and the Promised Land. The prophetic narrative concerning Israel is found in the great prophecies of Isaiah, Jeremiah, Ezekiel and Daniel with echoes in the minor prophets Joel, Hosea, Micah, and Zechariah. To this the New Testament adds little of importance, but these great prophecies not only trace the subsequent history of Egypt, much of which has now been fulfilled, but also paint the picture of the final chapter in relation to the second coming of Christ.

The Prophecies of Isaiah Concerning Egypt

The prophecies of Isaiah include one of the more important chapters of prophetic utterance concerning Egypt. The main section of this prophecy is found in the nineteenth chapter beginning with the ominous phrase, "the burden of Egypt." The chapter is preceded by prophecies relating to Egypt's neighbor Ethiopia and is followed in chapter 20 by the prediction that Assyria would conquer Egypt and Ethiopia and lead them off as captives.

The nineteenth chapter of Isaiah is of special interest because it provides a rather comprehensive picture of God's plan and purpose for Egypt. The first half of the chapter predicts divine judgment upon Egypt. This will be fulfilled by the destruction of their idols (verse 1), destruction by civil war followed by the rule of "a cruel lord" and "a fierce king" (verses 2-4), judgment on the Nile River with attending economic distress (verses 5-10), and confusion of their wise men (verses 11-15), accompanied by a dread of Jehovah (verse 16). Divine judgment can well be associated with events of the Old Testament period, although it may be a foreshadowing also of future judgments.

Beginning with verse 16, however, the thought seems gradually to change to that which will be fulfilled in the future. Although they will experience fear of Judah (verses 16-18), it is predicted that there will be "an altar to the LORD in the midst of the land of Egypt, and a pillar at the border thereof to the LORD" (verse 19). The passage which follows seems to anticipate a time of blessing which may have its ultimate fulfillment in the millennial reign of Christ. The thought is summarized in verse 22 in the phrase, "And the LORD shall smite Egypt: he shall smite and heal it: and they shall return even to the LORD, and he shall be intreated of them, and shall heal them." It is predicted that Egypt and Assyria will be associated with Israel as the three primary nations of that period and that a highway will connect them (verses 23, 24). The prophecies which follow in chapter 20 refer to the historic invasion of Egypt by Assyria fulfilled largely in Isaiah's day. Because of the ultimate downfall of Egypt, Israel is exhorted not to trust in Egypt as a refuge against other enemies (Isaiah 30:2, 3; 31:1; 36:6, 9). These prophecies assure God's continued attention to the nation Israel and His divine judgment upon them for their sins. From the standpoint of unfulfilled prophecy, the most important passage in Isaiah is found in 11:10-16. Here Egypt is mentioned as one of the nations from which Israel will be regathered (11:11).

One of the interesting predictions is found in Isaiah 11:15 where it states, "And the LORD shall utterly destroy the tongue of the Egyptian sea; and with his mighty wind shall he shake his hand over the river, and shall smite it in the seven streams, and make men go over dryshod." The passage then goes on to mention the highway between Assyria and Egypt also mentioned in Isaiah 19:23.

The interpretation depends largely on the question as to whether prophecy is to have literal fulfillment. Numerous attempts have been made to spiritualize these prophecies as referring to the progress of the church and conversion of the heathen. The more probable interpretation, however, is to take these as geographic terms and the events as those which will be related to the future Messianic kingdom. The tongue of the Egyptian Sea is clearly the northern end of the Red Sea. The prophecy then predicts that in this future time the topography of this land will be changed and what is now water will become dry land. This apparently is connected with the prophecy of a highway between Egypt and Israel for which this may be a preparation.

This passage with its prediction of Israel's future place is set in the midst of prophecy that refers to the future millennial kingdom on earth. The first part of chapter 11 deals with Christ's reign on earth in perfect righteousness and equity. Chapter 12 refers to the joy and blessings that will characterize worship in this kingdom. It must be concluded therefore not only that Israel will be revived and that a future kingdom on earth will be realized, but that many of the ancient nations mentioned in the Bible will have their future revival as well. As Isaiah the prophet makes so plain in chapter 2, Jerusalem will be the capital of the world and the nations surrounding Israel will be subordinate but nevertheless blessed of God in that day. Taken as a whole, the prophecies of Isaiah set the pattern for other portions of the Word of God in tracing precise fulfillment of many prophecies in the past already fulfilled and establishing the main outline of Israel's future in relationship to the earthly kingdom of the Messiah.

THE PROPHECIES OF JEREMIAH CONCERNING EGYPT

Most of the prophecies of Jeremiah concern Jeremiah's own generation and the struggles of the kingdom of Judah with the contending powers of Babylon and Egypt. The possibility of a Babylonian conquest precipitated the choice of either casting their lot with Egypt or submitting to the Babylonian armies. It was in this situation that Jeremiah the prophet delivered his prophetic message. The good king Josiah had been succeeded by his son Jehoiakim who was on the throne during the period in which Nebuchadnezzar was attempting to subdue Tyre — more than a dozen years. When Jehoiakim died, he was succeeded by his son Jehoiachin, who after three months was succeeded by Zedekiah, another son of Josiah and Jehoiachin's uncle. At this time Egypt was applying great pressure on the kingdom of Judah to cast their lot with them. When Jeremiah the prophet was consulted after receiving a message from God, he delivered his pronouncement as contained in Jeremiah 42. The substance of his reply was that they should not go down into Egypt and that if they did they would be destroyed. The advisors of king Zedekiah were intent, however, on going to Egypt and they rejected Jeremiah's prophetic warning and added insult to injury by forcing Jeremiah to accompany them as indicated in Jeremiah 43. While in Egypt Jeremiah delivered a further message to the Jews (chapter 44) predicting their destruction except for a small remnant that would escape and return to Israel. The eloquent and moving plea of Jeremiah is prophetic literature at its best and is highly significant because it embodies also complete and literal fulfillment.

Jeremiah continues his prophetic utterances concerning Egypt in the series of prophecies against the Gentiles beginning in chapter 46 and concluding with the great section against Babylon in chapter 50 and 51. In these predictions he anticipates the defeat of Egypt by Nebuchadnezzar and the destruction of their great cities. The section on Egypt concludes in chapter 46:27, 28 with another reminder to Israel that Jacob need not be afraid, that Israel would return from their captivity and ultimately be at rest and ease in their own land. As Jeremiah concluded, "Fear thou not, O Jacob my servant, saith the LORD: for I am with thee; for I will make a full end of all the nations whither I have driven thee: but I will not make a full end of thee, but correct thee in measure; yet will I not leave thee wholly unpunished" (Jeremiah 46:28). Taken as a whole, Jeremiah does not contribute much to the future of Egypt except to assure God's continued and providential direction of this nation to the fulfillment of His purpose to bring Israel into their ancient land and establish them in the millennial kingdom.

THE PROPHECIES OF EZEKIEL CONCERNING EGYPT

The prophecies of Ezekiel include four long chapters dealing with Egypt, beginning with the prophecy against Pharaoh in chapter 29. Most of these predictions are concerning the domination of Egypt by Babylon and Nebuchadnezzar viewed as a divine judgment of God upon Pharaoh for claiming to be God and taking the credit for the fertility of the Nile Valley. With great prophetic eloquence, Ezekiel declares that Egypt is going to fall even as Assyria fell more than a century before. Most of chapter 31 is devoted to the analogy between the fall of Assyria and the fall of Egypt. The concluding prophecy concerning Egypt is a lamentation contained in chapter 32 in which Egypt is compared to a young lion trapped with a net and destroyed.

In a similar way miscellaneous other prophecies in Ezekiel relate to the downfall of Egypt. In the parable of the great eagle in Ezekiel 17 and its interpretation, Ezekiel declares that the king of Babylon has conquered Jerusalem and will judge those who flee to Pharaoh for refuge. The foolishness of relying on Egypt is again mentioned in Ezekiel 19:4. Israel is likewise denounced for their wickedness in idol worship in Egypt in the parable of Aholah and

Aholibah representing Samaria and Jerusalem. God's judgment upon them for this is declared.

Of these many prophecies most of them related to the contemporary situation of Ezekiel's day. The opening portion of chapter 30 of Ezekiel, however, referring as it does to the day of the Lord, has been interpreted as having a dual fulfillment, first, in the conquest of Egypt and Ethiopia by Babylon and, second, the future conquest of Egypt in the world struggle which will end the age. The main burden of the prophecy, however, seems to relate to Nebuchadnezzar and his conquest as indicated in Ezekiel 30:10. Taken as a whole, Ezekiel is an enlargement of the prophecies of Isaiah and Jeremiah depicting the judgment upon Egypt in his day, but assuring the people of Israel of their ultimate restoration and deliverance.

THE PROPHECIES OF DANIEL CONCERNING EGYPT

To the prophet Daniel was committed the major task of tracing the prophetic program of the four great world empires, namely, Babylon, Medo-Persia, Greece, and Rome. This in the main is the times of the Gentiles, constituting one of the major programs of God. Under the circumstances, it is surprising that Daniel has so little to say specifically about Egypt.

In Daniel 9:15 there is an allusion in Daniel's prayer to the deliverance of the people of Israel out of the land of Egypt, a constantly recurring thought in the Old Testament. In Daniel 11:8 there is mention of captives being carried into Egypt, a reference to the supremacy of Egypt during the reign of Ptolemy III Euergetes (246-222 B.C.).

The two other references to Egypt are found in Daniel 11: 42, 43, and these relate to the future struggle among the nations at the end of the age still to be fulfilled.

The few direct references to Egypt, however, are misleading as Egypt figures in a large way in the events both historic and prophetic described in Daniel chapter 11. Instead of referring to Egypt by name reference is made instead to "the king of the south," an expression which occurs in Daniel 11:5, 6, 9, 11, 14, 15, 25, 29, 40, a total of ten references including the double reference in 11:25. Instead of referring to only one ruler, however, the expression in all probability concerns seven different kings of Egypt, six of them in the past and one still to come.

The period of history described in Daniel 11:5-20 was the tangled period subsequent to the death of Alexander the Great which deals with the struggles of Egypt with the lands to the north, principally Syria. The accuracy of the prophecy given by Daniel more than two hundred years before it was fulfilled is so minute that liberal scholars reject the idea that Daniel could possibly have written it and claim it was written by a pseudo-Daniel after the events had actually taken place. Evangelical scholarship, however, has been agreed that this is genuine prophecy and another illustration of the accuracy of the prophetic Word.

The king of the south mentioned in Daniel 11:5 was probably Ptolemy I Soter (323-285 B.C.) who was associated with the famous Seleucus I Nicator (312-281 B.C.) who was king of Babylon. Their alliance succeeded in defeating Antigonus and Seleucus I Nicator became the ruler of the entire area from Asia Minor to India and hence was stronger than Ptolemy I Soter, his associate.

The king of the south mentioned in Daniel 11:6 was probably Ptolemy II Philadelphus (283-246 B.C. who gave his daughter Berenice to Antiochus II Theos (261-246 B.C.) who was the third in the line of Seleucid kings.

Reference to another king of Egypt is found in verses 7 and 8. He was probably Ptolemy II Euergetes (246-222 B.C.) referred to as the king of the south in Daniel 11:9. The king of the south of Daniel 11:11 was Ptolemy IV Philopator (222-203 B.C.). The king of the south mentioned in verse 14 and referred to under the term "the arms of the south" in verse 15 was Ptolemy V Epiphanes (204-181 B.C.) who was an infant at the time of his accession. As Daniel 11:13-16 indicates, he was crushed by the great army of Antiochus III the celebrated ruler of Syria to the north in a battle at Paneiom in 198 B.C. The result was that Egypt lost its hold upon the Holy Land and it was transferred to the Seleucids. This set the stage for the activities of Antiochus Epiphanes described in Daniel 11:21-35 (previously discussed) which constitutes such a significant foreshadowing of the coming man of sin and world ruler in the end time. Antiochus III was followed by his son Seleucus IV Philopator (187-175 B.C.) to whom reference is made in Daniel 11:20 as a raiser of taxes. He was followed in turn by Antiochus Epiphanes.

The exact fulfillment of these many prophecies, including that of Antiochus Epiphanes in Daniel 11:21-35, sets the stage for the climactic prophecy beginning in Daniel 11:36 which leaps the centuries to the end of the age and the final king of Gentile power.

Daniel 11:36-45 concerns itself with the military and political struggles of the end of the age with special reference to the great tribulation the last three and a half years before the second coming of Christ to the earth. The period is described as "the time of the end" in verse 35 and again in Daniel 11:40. The description of the warfare which characterizes the period of Daniel 11:40-45 speaks of a future king of the south, namely, of Egypt engaging in a military campaign against the king of Daniel 11:36 who is most probably identified as the world ruler of the end time. At the same time there is an attack by the king of the north, namely, Russia and her associates as they contend with the world ruler for control of the Holy Land.

It is reasonable to assume from the description of a series of battles that this is not just one single military encounter, but a series of military maneuvers which come at the very end of the great tribulation. Earlier there may have been other wars such as that of Ezekiel 38 and 39 which led up to the world empire directed by the head of the revived Roman Empire. With the defeat of Russia described in Ezekiel 38 and 39, however, the Roman ruler becomes a world ruler. His empire accomplished by proclamation and because there was no suitable military force to contend against him does not stand indefinitely, however, and begins to fall apart with a major rebellion developing as the great tribulation closes. This is the scene described in Daniel 11:40 and following.

According to Daniel 11:40-42 the preliminary struggle results in the Roman ruler being victorious and conquering Egypt and putting down the king of the south. In the process, however, of assuming "power over the treasures of gold and of silver, and over all the precious things of Egypt" (Daniel 11:43) he receives word of additional problems of a military force coming from the east and from the north. This apparently refers to the great host coming from the Orient described first in Revelation 9:13-21, an army of two hundred million and then again in a later phase in the invasion described in Revelation 16:12-16. The great invasion from the east therefore follows the attack of the king of the south. Daniel 11, however, makes plain that in the preliminary struggle the Roman ruler is victorious as indicated in Daniel 11:45. However, at the very time of the second coming of Christ according to Zechariah chapter 14:1-3 a military struggle is going on in the city of Jerusalem itself and the armies of the world are gathered in the Holy Land with the valley of Megiddo referred to as Armageddon (Revelation 16:16) as its marshalling center.

From this entire context it is evident that the king of the south, namely, Egypt, has a part in end-time events and participates in the world struggle leading up to the second coming of Christ.

However, a final chapter is written in Egypt's future in which it is pictured that Egypt will have a spiritual revival (cp. Isaiah 19:18-24) and Israel will be regathered.

PROPHECIES OF EGYPT IN THE MINOR PROPHETS

The few scattered references to Egypt in the minor prophets do not contribute much to the total picture. Hosea has the most references, including the Messianic statement in Hosea 11:1: "When Israel was a child, then I loved him, and called my son out of Egypt." This reference to the Exodus is interpreted as having a dual meaning in that it prophesies that Jesus would come out of Egypt (cp. Matthew 2:15). Other references to Egypt in Hosea either predict destruction of those who go to Egypt as in Hosea 7: 11-16 or contain warnings concerning returning to Egypt as in 8: 13; 9:3, 6; 11:5. Joel 3:19 predicts that "Egypt shall be a desolation." This seems to be a general reference to God's judgment on Egypt largely already fulfilled although it is found in a passage dealing with Israel's millennial blessings.

Micah in one reference (7:12) predicts the regathering of Israel from Assyria and from "the fortress." This is best interpreted as a reference to Egypt and hence the prediction is that the children of Israel will be gathered from Assyria, the cities of Egypt ("the fortified cities"), and from Egypt ("the fortress") even to the river (the Euphrates). This reference to regathering from Egypt may presume an influx of Jews into Egypt which is not true today or it may refer to the few that are there as being subject to regathering.

The subject of regathering is brought up again in Zechariah 10:10 where it is stated concerning Israel, "I will bring them again also out of the land of Egypt, and gather them out of Assyria." Zechariah 10:11 refers to the fact that both Assyria and Egypt will be afflicted under divine judgment in contrast to God's blessing upon Israel.

The final reference in the Old Testament to Egypt is found in

Zechariah 14:18, 19, where in the future millennial kingdom it is stated, "And if the family of Egypt go not up, and come not, that have no rain; there shall be the plague, wherewith the LORD will smite the heathen that come not up to keep the feast of tabernacles. This shall be the punishment of Egypt, and the punishment of all nations that come not up to keep the feast of tabernacles." From these verses it may be concluded that God will continue to discipline Egypt even in the coming millennial kingdom if they have failed to obey Him and observe His feast.

SUMMARY

Taking the Scriptural prophecies concerning Egypt as a whole, it is easily seen that Egypt has had a great role as one of the principal neighbors of Israel in centuries past. The fact that Israel sojourned in Egypt, grew to be a great nation there and subsequently had so many dealings with Egypt forms a large part of the Old Testament prophetic narrative.

The Scriptures, however, reveal that Egypt will also have a place in the future. Egypt will be one of the nations which figure in the final world conflict and will be the leader of the African forces in contending against the Roman ruler who is attempting to maintain a world empire. The role of Egypt will continue in the millennial kingdom after the searching divine judgments which attend the second coming. The last word of the Old Testament pictures the continued discipline of Egypt in the millennium if they fail to observe the rule of the king.

Chapter XII

THE KINGS OF THE EAST:
THE ORIENTAL CONFEDERACY

One of the significant developments of the twentieth century is the political and military awakening of the Orient. The great nations of Asia east of the Euphrates River, slumbering for centuries, are now beginning to stir and to become a major factor in the international situation. The geographic immensity and the millions of humanity involved make it inevitable that any future development embracing the entire world must take the Orient into consideration.

In our twentieth century the major nations of Asia have thrown off the yoke of political overlordship of western civilization. Red China with its population approaching one billion is flexing its muscles not only against the United States of America, but even against its associate in communism, Russia. India, now independent of Great Britain, is likewise beginning to feel its strength. Japan is experiencing a great industrial revolution where the comforts and manufacturing techniques of western civilization are now an integral part of Japanese life. Lesser nations also are beginning to assert themselves, hoping for a large role in world affairs. Most of this has taken place in the last twenty-five years and developments continue to be rapid. Even if there were no Scripture bearing on the place of the Orient in end-time events, it would be only natural to expect them to be part of the world-wide scene.

The great nations of Eastern Asia have had no important part in the history of Israel. Far removed in geography and interests, there is no record of any past war between Israel and the nations beyond the Euphrates. Alexander the Great penetrated as far as India with his armies, but he left no permanent imprint upon the oriental world. The future, however, in view of modern rapid communications and transportation and the world-wide character of any military effort in the missile age, will be a different story.

The western world was rudely awakened to the power of the Orient by the Japanese attack on Pearl Harbor on December 7, 1941. During the months that followed, the Japanese army, navy, and air force dominated the Asiatic scene. It was only when the full force of American military power was brought into play that Japan went down along with its ally, Germany. The downfall of Japan, however, was followed by the emergence of Red China and independent India. The conflict between the United States and Viet Nam, although not large in extent, symbolizes that Asia is the number one problem of the world today.

In World War II the Japanese Yamamoto was quoted as boasting, "I shall not be content merely to occupy Guam, the Philippines, Hawaii, and San Francisco. I shall look forward to dictating peace to the United States in the White House at Washington." Although today this is an idle boast, Red China and Russia are still dreaming of world conquest by means of communistic philosophy. No one takes lightly the possibility of a world-wide conflict sparked by the belligerence of Red China and other communistic nations. In this confused situation that has so many omens of future disaster for western civilization, a student of the Scriptures may well ask whether prophecy has any sure word concerning the role of Asia among the nations of the world in the end time.

CHINA IN PROPHECY

Scriptures rarely go outside the confines of the ancient Roman Empire in predicting future events. An exception to this is the statement found in Isaiah 49:12 relating to the ultimate regathering of the nation Israel, "Behold, these shall come from far: and, lo, these from the north and from the west; and these from the land of Sinim." Although it is not possible to be dogmatic as to the precise reference of "the land of Sinim," conservative scholarship has generally agreed that the most probable explanation is that this refers to the ancient land of China.

It is known that China for centuries was a great nation and had its own culture and extensive history long before Christ was born in Bethlehem. It is possible to trace some commercial relationships with China in ancient days as far as the Mediterranean and there is also evidence that some of the history of the Old Testament was known in China. Even if the Chinese had not penetrated as far west as the Mediterranean, the world-wide scattering of the people of Israel would inevitably have brought some of them to the great land of China. Under these circumstances, the prophecy assumes a logical and natural interpretation, namely, that in the end time some of the Jews who will be regathered will come not only from the north and the west, the more important directions of concentration of Jewish population, but also from the east. Although this prophecy is not related to events which concern the nations, it does indicate that the Scriptures recognize the existence of the Far East in relation to the Holy Land.

THE MAGI FROM THE EAST

One of the most familiar Biblical references to the Far East is related to the visit of the Magi as they brought gifts to the Christ child. According to Matthew 2:1, 2, "Now when Jesus was born in Bethlehem of Judaea in the days of Herod the king, behold, there came wise men from the east to Jerusalem, Saying, Where is he that is born King of the Jews? for we have seen his star in the east, and are come to worship him."

It has been commonly held from the times of the early church fathers that these strange visitors came from the area east of the Euphrates and probably from ancient Persia. The Persian origin of the Magi was suggested by such men as Clement of Alexandria, Diodorus of Tarsus, Chrysostom, and Cyril of Alexandria. Somehow the Messianic hope had been transmitted in some form even to this distant land. The star appearing over Bethlehem prompted their journey and inquiry concerning the birth of the King of the Jews. The fact that they wanted to worship Him and recognized Him as the King of the Jews reveals that the basic facts concerning the Old Testament were more widely known than is commonly realized. As in the case of the reference to the land of Sinim, the story in the New Testament gives added support to the conclusion that the Bible includes the Orient in its world-wide view.

DANIEL'S PROPHECY OF A MILITARY INVASION FROM THE FAR EAST

In Daniel's prophecy of "the time of the end" beginning in Daniel 11:35, a king is pictured in the Mediterranean area who engages in a military conflict with the king of the south, the king of the north, and a military force from the east. Although identification of this king is difficult, the most plausible explanation is that he is the head of the revived Roman Empire who at this point has assumed the role of a world dictator. In the period just prior to the second coming of Christ in the latter part of the great tribulation, major portions of the world will rebel against him. This explains the military conflict with armies pushing against him from the south, the north, and from the east.

In the prophecy it is stated in Daniel 11:44, "But tidings out of the east and out of the north shall trouble him: therefore he shall go forth with great fury to destroy, and utterly to make away many." Although the information given is meager, in the light of the context it appears that these tidings concern a military invasion from the Orient. This is probably the first word of trouble in the Orient in relation to his world-wide empire and comes as an added blow to insurrection in the north and the south. It appears that he is victorious in his preliminary battles with the north and the south, as it states in Daniel 11:44, "therefore he shall go forth with great fury to destroy, and utterly to make away many." But that the conflict is not completely resolved, is borne out by the fact that at the time of the second coming of Christ a great war is under way in which the armies are deployed over much of the Holy Land with the valley of Armageddon as its focal point. The statement in Daniel, however, introduces a subject concerning which there is additional revelation given in the New Testament that lends support to the concept that the Orient will have a place in the great world conflict of the end time.

THE GREAT ARMY FROM THE ORIENT

Two important passages in Revelation, namely, 9:13-21 and 16:12-16 contribute to the conclusion that one of the large armies employed in the final world conflict will be a military force of great power which comes from the Orient. The first intimation of this is found in Revelation 9 where it is recorded that John

> heard a voice from the four horns of the golden altar which is before God, Saying to the sixth angel which had the trumpet, Loose the four angels which are bound in the great river Euphrates, And the four angels were loosed, which were prepared for an hour, and a day, and a month, and a year, for to slay the third part of men. And the number of the army of the horsemen were two hundred thousand thousand: and I heard the number of them (verses 13-16).

The passage goes on to describe the character of this army and the conclusion that one-third of the men were killed in the resulting military struggle.

Although all of the details are not entirely clear, the most reasonable explanation of this prophecy, related as it is to the great river Euphrates which forms the eastern boundary of the ancient Roman Empire, is that the army comes from the Orient and crosses the Euphrates River in order to participate in the struggle that is going on in the land of Israel. The information that it is prepared for "an hour, and a day, and a month, and a year, for to slay the third part of men" means simply that it is an army especially prepared for the day of battle which follows.

A most staggering statistic is the fact that the number of the horsemen is declared to be two hundred thousand thousand or two hundred million. Never in the history of the human race until now has there been an army of this size. The total number of men under arms in World War II on both sides of the conflict together never was more than fifty million. Accordingly, it has been the custom for expositors to spiritualize the number or to regard the army as demonic rather than human. The statistics of two hundred million horsemen must have been especially astounding to the Apostle John for at that time the total world population did not exceed this number. With the twentieth century and its attendant population explosion, however, the number of an army of two hundred milion men becomes increasingly a possibility and with modern transportation and means of supply, for the first time in history such an army is plausible. It is at least of more than passing interest that Red China alone claims to have a man and woman militia engaging in serious training numbering two hundred million (*Time*, May 21, 1965, page 35), precisely the figure mentioned in Revelation 9:16.

Although their militia includes the home guard which under present circumstances would not be thrown into a battle such as the one in Revelation, it at least introduces the possibility that the number should be taken literally. If so, this is an imposing statistic of the power and influence of the Orient in the final world war. The deadly character of the army is revealed in their slaughter of one third, a figure mentioned in Revelation 9:15 and again in Revelation 9:18. Although it may not be intended to consider this as one third of the entire world's population, the implication is that many millions of people are involved.

THE KINGS OF THE EAST

A later development in prophetic fulfillment is portrayed in the sixth vial described in Revelation 16:12-16. There it is recorded, "And the sixth angel poured out his vial upon the great river Euphrates; and the water thereof was dried up, that the way of the kings of the east might be prepared" (Revelation 16:12). Revelation 16:14 reveals that this movement is part of a world-wide gathering of "the kings of the earth and of the whole world" in order that they might participate in "the battle of that great day of God Almighty." The focal point of the gathering is mentioned as Armageddon in Revelation 16:16.

Many interpretations have arisen concerning the meaning of the phrase "the kings of the east." These interpretations may be divided into two classes, those that take this phrase literally, and those who find in it a nonliteral meaning. If the nonliteral interpretation be followed there is no end to the possible interpretation. The kings of the east have been connected with almost every important set of characters in the world. The bewildering array of conflicting opinions is its own refutation.

The kings of the east have been identified with the Dacians who conquered Rome and the Euphrates is then taken to represent the Danube. Others relate the kings of the east to the Parthians who contended against Rome at the Euphrates. Some have referred it to the people of Israel returning to their ancient land or identified it with the kingdom of God or Christianity. Some think it refers to the ten kings of Revelation 17:12; others have related it to the Apostles or to the four angels of Revelation 9:14, 15. Still other explanations have been given such as relating it to Vitringa, or Constantine the Great, or to Gog and Magog, or Turkey, and still other interpretations too numerous to mention. A method of interpretation yielding so many different results is obviously wrong in principle.

The most simple and suitable explanation is to take the passage literally. The Euphrates River then becomes the geographic boundary of the ancient Roman Empire. The kings of the east are kings from the east or "of the sunrising," that is, monarchs who originated in the Orient. The battle which ensues is therefore a genuine military conflict.

THE DRYING UP OF THE EUPHRATES RIVER

The interpretation of this difficult passage, if taken literally, provides an important segment of information concerning the final world conflict. The prophecy begins with a reference to the Euphrates River and the declaration that "the water thereof was dried up." Just what is meant?

From the standpoint of Scripture, the Euphrates River is one of the important rivers of the world. The first reference is found in Genesis 2:10-14 where it is included as one of the four rivers having its source in the garden of Eden. The Euphrates River is mentioned a total of nineteen times in the Old Testament and twice in the New Testament. In Genesis 15:18 it is cited as the eastern boundary of the land promised to Israel. An army, therefore, which crosses the Euphrates River from the east to the west by this act invades the Promised Land.

The Euphrates River is important in some of the major events of the Bible. Although not mentioned by name in Daniel 5, it was the diversion of the Euphrates River from its normal course through the midst of Babylon that left the river channel dry and permitted the armies of Darius the Mede to take the city by storm on the memorable night of Belshazzar's feast (Daniel 5). Therefore the drying up of the Euphrates contributed to the downfall of Babylon. There seems to be a connotation in that the drying of the Euphrates River in Revelation 16:12 will lead to the downfall of the revived Roman Empire which spiritually and politically is also identified with Babylon.

The drying up of the Euphrates, however, is probably best interpreted as a literal but miraculous drying up of the Euphrates River thereby permitting easy access of the military hordes from the Orient to cross its dry river bed. The Euphrates River has long been an important geographic barrier and in the ancient world was second to none in importance. Its total length was some seventeen hundred miles, and it was the main river of southwestern Asia dividing the land geographically much as the Mississippi River divides North America. Not only from the standpoint of prophecy, but historically, geographically, and biblically the Euphrates River is the most important in the ancient world. To take it literally is therefore not a strange or an unnatural conclusion.

The drying up of the Euphrates is pictured as an act of God. This has inspired all sorts of nonliteral interpretations as symbolizing some great victory of God. In the past this has been suggestive of the declining power of Turkey, or as anticipating a future decline in the Roman Catholic Church. Although Turkey has receded in power, there is no evidence that this applies to Rome or any other ecclesiastical organization. It is rather a physical act permitting the army to cross the Euphrates much as was enacted in God drying up the waters of the Red Sea and of the Jordan to permit the passage of the children of Israel without difficulty. Inasmuch as such a literal interpretation makes a great deal of sense and there is no agreement as to the spiritualized meaning of the passage, the literal interpretation is obviously to be preferred.

If the drying of the Euphrates River is to be taken literally, then what can be understood by the reference to "the kings of the east"? Here again the literal view is to be preferred. Inasmuch as it would be most natural in a world war culminating in the Middle East to have the Orient represented, the interpretation that views the kings of the east as the political and military leaders of Asiatic forces east of the Euphrates is a satisfactory solution.

There has been some tendency to take the expression "the kings of the east" — literally, "the kings of the sunrise" — as referring specifically to Japan where the rising sun is a symbol of its political power. However, it is more natural to consider the term "rising sun" as a synonym for east, and therefore the army would include all the nations of the Orient. If the army is literally two hundred million, it would hardly be possible for Japan alone to staff, maintain, and move such a gigantic force without help from China, India, and other great nations of the Orient.

CONCLUSION

The ultimate explanation is therefore relatively a simple one. By an act of God the Euphrates River is dried up. This makes easy the descent of the tremendous army of two hundred million men upon the land of Israel to participate in the final world conflict. If such an army is to be raised up, it would be natural to conclude that it would come from Asia, the great population center of the world. Although they seem to come in opposition to the Roman ruler and his power, it is clear that this invasion springs from unbelief and these armies like the others gathered "to the battle of that great day of God Almighty" forget their individual conflicts to oppose the coming of Jesus Christ in power and glory from heaven.

The fact that the rise of Asia has occurred in our twentieth century with so many rapid and unexpected developments is another evidence that the world is moving toward its final climax and the end of the times of the Gentiles. In Asia, as in other parts of the world, the stage is being set for the final drama in which the kings of the east will have their important part.

CHAPTER XIII

ARMAGEDDON AND THE SECOND COMING OF CHRIST

The dramatic conclusion of the "times of the Gentiles" is described in prophecy as a gigantic world war which is climaxed by the second coming of Christ. The war that brings to a close the times of the Gentiles, which already has embraced twenty-five hundred years of history, is also the final effort of Satan in his strategy of opposition to the divine program of God. The second coming of Christ is God's answer. Some of the major elements of this conflict have already been considered and now need only to be related one to the other.

THE BEGINNING OF THE FINAL WORLD CONFLICT

The great world war which will engulf the Middle East at the end of the age is an outgrowth of the world situation during the time of the great tribulation. The Roman Empire formed earlier has now extended its power "over all kindreds, and tongues, and nations" (Revelation 13:7). The world government formed at the beginning of the great tribulation is scheduled in prophecy to endure for forty-two months or three and a half years (Revelation 13:5). At its beginning there is no serious challenge of the power and authority of the world ruler, and he is able to assume supreme power not only in the political field, but also receives recognition and worship as God and controls the economic power of the entire world. His reign is afflicted, however, by a series of great judgments of God described in the breaking of the seals, the blowing of the trumpets, and the outpouring of the vials of the wrath of God (Revelation 6:1—18:24). The disruptive force of these judgments is keenly felt throughout the world and it soon becomes evident that the promised utopia which his rule was designed to produce is not going to be fulfilled.

THE TRINITY OF EVIL

Many students of prophecy have noted the "trinity of evil" which characterizes the end time. In some respects this trinity corresponds to the Trinity of the Godhead. The ultimate source of power and evil in the end time is none other than Satan himself, referred to as "the great dragon," and as "that old serpent, called the Devil, and Satan" (Revelation 12:9). The political as well as the religious power which dominates the world is unquestionably Satan, and for this reason it is stated in Revelation 13:4 that the world "worshipped the dragon which gave power unto the beast." Satan assumes much the same power and prerogatives as God the Father.

The world ruler, who is Satan's masterpiece as a counterfeit of Christ, is the actual supreme dictator of the entire world and in a sense is Satan incarnate. He is undoubtedly a brilliant man intellectually and a dynamic personality, but he is completely dominated by Satan. In keeping with the satanic approach of imitation and counterfeit of God's program, the world ruler is Satan's king of kings and lord of lords. Many students of Scripture assign the term "antichrist" to this person for this reason, although in the Bible none of the references to antichrist clearly indicate the personage in view (cp. I John 2:18, 22; 4:3; II John 7).

The third member of the unholy trinity is the "beast coming up out of the earth" (Revelation 13:11) who assists the world ruler, performing satanic miracles and causing all men to worship the image of the beast (Revelation 13:12-15). He apparently also is instrumental in linking the economic and religious life of the world in that only those who worship the beast can buy or sell (Revelation 13:16). This personage is undoubtedly the same as "the false prophet" (Revelation 19:20) and in every respect he is the right-hand man and expediter for the world ruler. In his activities he corresponds to some extent to the ministry of the Holy Spirit on behalf of Christ and thus forms the third member of the trinity of evil. The world situation is therefore firmly in the grasp of Satan, Satan's man who is the world dictator, and the false prophet who heads up the satanic world religion of the great tribulation. In spite of the satanic control of the world by divine plan (Revelation 16:16), as the great tribulation moves on to its close, major sections of the world rebel against their ruler, and this sets the stage for the final great world war.

THE GATHERING OF THE ARMIES OF THE WORLD

The armies of the world which converge upon the Middle East according to Revelation 16:13 are induced to engage in the final conflict by satanic influences. This is introduced in the statement of John the Apostle: "I saw three unclean spirits like frogs come out of the mouth of the dragon, and out of the mouth of the beast, and out of the mouth of the false prophet. For they are the spirits of devils, working miracles, which go forth unto the kings of the earth and of the whole world, to gather them to the battle of that great day of God Almighty" (Revelation 16:13, 14).

There has been endless speculation as to the identity of the three unclean spirits like frogs. The passage itself indicates plainly that they are spirits of devils or demons and unquestionably are fallen angels under the command of Satan who are sent forth to draw the kings of the world into this final conflict. Humanly speaking, they are gathering to wrest the world rulership from the Roman ruler. In the satanic purpose, however, the armies of the world are gathered to fight the armies of heaven which will accompany Christ at His second coming. As in so many undertakings of Satan, such as is supremely illustrated in the crucifixion of Christ, the very program of Satan is its own destruction, and although Satan is inevitably impelled to gigantic opposition to Christ, he only sets the stage for the triumph of God. It is to facilitate the gathering of these armies that the Euphrates River is dried up that the armies from the east may converge without difficulty upon the Middle East.

Three major armies are mentioned in the Bible, namely, the army from the north, the army from the east, and the army from the south. These three armies are combining their efforts to wrest power from the Roman ruler who may be considered as the king of the west, although this title is never given to him in the Scriptures. The focal point for their gathering is declared in Revelation 16:16 to be "a place called in the Hebrew tongue Armageddon." Although various explanations have been given of this title, it seems to refer to the valley of Esdraelon also known as the valley of Jezreel located to the east of Megiddo in northern Israel. The word *Armageddon* actually means Mount of Megiddo from *har* meaning mount and Megiddo.

The broad valley that is here described is approximately fourteen miles wide and twenty miles long and historically has been the scene of many great battles of the past. In modern times the area became a great swamp, but with the revival of the area under the state of Israel the water has now been drained, and it is a fruitful and beautiful plain well suited for a great army. It is obvious, however, that this is only the central staging area for the war as actually the size of the armies involved preclude the possibility of confining them to this valley. As Scripture indicates, the war rages for some two hundred miles north and south thereby engulfing the entire Holy Land.

THE EARLY BATTLES OF THE FINAL WORLD WAR

Scripture does not provide much detail on the characteristics of the final world conflict. The main significance is that they are assembled in the Holy Land at the time of the second advent and oppose Christ in His return to the earth. However, some indication of the nature of the battles preceding the second coming of Christ is given in Daniel 11:40-45. If the order of introduction of events is taken chronologically, it appears that the first stage of the battle is an attack by the king of the south. According to Daniel 11:40, "And at the time of the end shall the king of the south push at him."

In rapid succession an attack also comes from the north which apparently is successful. The Scriptures state that "the king of the north shall come against him like a whirlwind, with chariots, and with horsemen, and with many ships; and he shall enter into the countries, and shall overflow and pass over." This king of the north may be Russia. The force of his invasion is such that he proceeds through the Holy Land and conquers Egypt at least temporarily. (Some expositors, however, interpret the passage beginning in Daniel 11:42 as referring to the Roman ruler who is naturally to the north of Africa, rather than to Russia as the king of the north, i.e., north of Palestine, as this seems to be the main theme of the passage.) The warfare brought about by the invasion of the king of the north and the king of the south, however, is now followed by another phase, namely, the arrival of the host from the east.

According to Daniel 11:44, "Tidings out of the east and out of the north shall trouble him: therefore he shall go forth with great fury to destroy, and utterly to make away many." The arrival of the forces from the Orient described as an army of two hundred million in Revelation 9:16 brings on the last phase of the world struggle, and at the time of the second coming of Christ the war is raging in a number of areas.

At least four geographic locations are mentioned in the Bible as figuring in the final struggle. The center, of course, is Armageddon where the main forces are located. Another focal point for the battle is the city of Jerusalem itself. According to Zechariah 12:2-10 a siege will be declared against the city of Jerusalem. Jerusalem apparently will be defended to some extent by the power of God by miraculous intervention, for the armies of the world have great difficulty in subduing the city. It is stated in Zechariah 12:3, "And in that day will I make Jerusalem a burdensome stone for all people: all that burden themselves with it shall be cut in pieces, though all the people of the earth be gathered together against it." The passage goes on to say how the horses are smitten with blindness and the riders with madness.

At the time of the second coming of Christ, however, Jerusalem has finally been entered and is in the process of being subdued at the very moment that the glory of Christ in the heavens in His second advent appears. This is stated in Zechariah 14:2, 3: "For I will gather all nations against Jerusalem to battle; and the city shall be taken, and the houses rifled, and the women ravished; and half of the city shall go forth into captivity, and the residue of the people shall not be cut off from the city. Then shall the LORD go forth, and fight against those nations, as when he fought in the day of battle." From this description it is clear that the nations are engaged in active warfare in relation to Jerusalem at the time of the second advent.

Another geographic location is that of the valley of Jehoshaphat mentioned in Joel 3:2, 12. Although there is some dispute as to its location, it appears to be a valley immediately east of Jerusalem. Here, according to Joel, God declares: "I will also gather all nations, and will bring them down into the valley of Jehoshaphat, and will plead with them there for my people and for my heritage Israel, whom they have scattered among the nations, and parted my land." This valley is the scene of the divine judgment mentioned in Joel 3:12. Whether this gathering has to do with the battle for Jerusalem or is a subsequent event to the second advent, is not entirely clear.

Still another geographic location mentioned is that of Edom in Isaiah 34:1-6 and 63:1-6. Again it is not entirely clear, however, whether this is part of the battle or a subsequent judgment of God. In Daniel 11:41 Edom, Moab, and Ammon are specifically mentioned as escaping the full brunt of the battle.

The awful bloodshed stemming from this conflict is indicated in Revelation 9:18 where one-third of the armies are declared to be destroyed by the army from the east and the statement in Revelation 14:20 that "blood came out of the winepress, even unto the horse bridles, by the space of a thousand and six hundred furlongs." This is a distance of approximately two hundred miles and seems to indicate the extent of the bloody battle as these armies converge upon the Holy Land.

Although the exact deployment of the forces and the precise character of the successive battles which precede the second coming of Christ are not indicated in Scripture, it is sufficient for us to know that the Holy Land will be crowded with the armies of the world in preparation for the dramatic second advent of Christ. This is the final showdown of Gentile power dominated by Satan in blasphemous opposition to the Lordship of Jesus Christ.

THE SECOND COMING OF CHRIST AND THE ANNIHILATION OF THE ARMIES

As the armies of the world are engaged in struggle for power throughout the Holy Land and in the very act of sacking the city of Jerusalem, the glory of the Lord appears in heaven and the majestic procession pictured in Revelation 19:11-16 takes place. At the head of the procession is Christ, described as riding on a white horse coming to judge and make war. His eyes are as a flame of fire and on His head are many crowns. His vesture is dipped in blood. Accompanying Him are the armies of heaven also riding on white horses and clothed in fine linen. In verse 15 it is stated of Christ, "Out of his mouth goeth a sharp sword, that with it he should smite the nations: and he shall rule them with a rod of iron: and he treadeth the winepress of the fierceness and wrath of Almighty God."

In contrast to His lowly birth in Bethlehem where He was laid in a manger, this advent is the triumphant King of kings and Lord of lords coming to claim the world for which He died and over which He is now going to exercise His sovereign authority in absolute power. The verses which follow invite the fowls of the earth to feed upon the carnage of the flesh of kings and mighty men and of their horses (Revelation 19:18).

According to Revelation 19:19 the armies of the world, which have previously been fighting each other, forget their differences and unite to fight against Christ in His second advent to the earth. John writes: "I saw the beast, and the kings of the earth, and their armies, gathered together to make war against him that sat on the horse, and against his army." Their struggle against such an adversary, however, is useless. It is apparent that they are put to death not by ordinary military struggle, but by the word of authority proceeding out of His mouth described as "a sharp sword" (Revelation 19:15). All the armies and their horses apparently are put to death at one stroke, but the beast (the world ruler) and the false prophet (the religious ruler of the world) are taken alive, and according to Revelation 19:20, "These both were cast alive into a lake of fire burning with brimstone." However, the doom of the rest is sealed in Revelation 19:21: "And the remnant were slain with the sword of him that sat upon the horse, which sword proceeded out of his mouth: and all the fowls were filled with their flesh."

Thus ends in one dramatic blow the power of the Gentiles which had controlled Jerusalem from the time of Nebuchadnezzar, 606 B.C. Thus ends also the satanic control of the Gentiles who had been a demonstration of satanic power, guilty of blasphemy and of the blood of countless martyrs, especially in oppressing the nation Israel.

Satan, their unseen leader, is also dealt with, and according to Revelation 20:1-3 he is cast into the abyss where he is rendered inactive for the entire period of the thousand-year reign of Christ on earth. Then he is destined to join the beast and the false prophet in the lake of fire (Revelation 20:10). The Gentile population of the world as a whole is judged at a separate judgment which follows and is a part of the establishment of Christ's kingdom on earth.

The inglorious end of Gentile power is precisely that which was anticipated in Daniel 2 where the great image disintegrates into chaff when struck by the stone cut out without hands. The same dramatic end is contemplated in the destruction of the beast (Daniel 7:11) followed by the inauguration of the everlasting kingdom in Daniel 7:13, 14. Jerusalem was no longer to be trodden under the feet of the Gentiles and once again Israel was to be exalted.

CHAPTER XIV

THE JUDGMENT OF THE NATIONS

In the broad program of divine dealings with the Gentiles, the sovereignty of God over creation is revealed in an unusual way. Although God in His sovereign grace has allowed Gentiles to assume great power and in the words of Christ, "Jerusalem shall be trodden down of the Gentiles, until the times of the Gentiles be fulfilled" (Luke 21:24), the consummation of this program inevitably brings the Gentiles before God for much-deserved divine judgment.

The history of the world has demonstrated that mankind is not judged once but many times. God has already exercised His judgment upon angels, Adam and Eve, and many particular judgments have fallen upon individuals, cities, and nations. In the flood of Noah the entire world was subject to disciplinary judgment. Towering above all judgments in history is the fact that Christ on the cross was judged as the sin bearer for mankind and that there Satan also was judged and defeated (John 16:11). Christians in this present age of grace also experience the disciplinary judgment of God (I Corinthians 11:32). Throughout the whole period of the tribulation and especially in the great tribulation judgment after judgment is poured out upon the world.

In this sequence the judgment of the nations assumes great significance and is one of the important milestones in divine dealing with a wicked world. That it is not the final judgment is evident, for other judgments will follow at the end of the millennium and the final judgment of all will be at the Great White Throne. The judgment of the nations, however, is important as bringing to a close one of the major phases of divine dealings, namely, the times of the Gentiles, and in a preliminary way anticipates the judgment of all unsaved men which will occur a thousand years later. The confusion which has arisen in the attempt to make this

the judgment of all men, including both the resurrected and translated saints as well as the wicked, is corrected by careful attention
to the exact text of Matthew 25:31-46 where the details of the
judgment are given.

THE TIME OF THE JUDGMENT

The passage is introduced by a time clause indicating when
the judgment will take place in the tremendous sequence of events
related to the second coming: "When the Son of man shall come in
his glory" (Matthew 25:31). The context indicates that this is the
coming of Christ to the earth in connection with the establishment
of His earthly kingdom. The judgment, therefore, is distinguished
in time from judgments that relate to the judgment seat of Christ
occurring in connection with the rapture of the church, and from
all historic judgments that precede as well as the many judgments
that are poured upon the earth during the great tribulation. It
follows the second coming of Christ to the earth, and precedes and
is a preparation for His reign on earth for a thousand years. Therefore it is also distinguished from any judgments on rebellion during
His kingdom reign and from the final judgment of the Great White
Throne at the end of the millennium.

THE PLACE OF THE JUDGMENT

From the context it is also clear that the place of the judgment
is earth, not heaven. The phrase, "the Son of man shall come in his
glory, and all the holy angels with him," is a picture of Christ and
the angels coming from heaven to the earth. This is substantiated
by another time clause, "Then shall he sit upon the throne of his
glory" (Matthew 25:31). This is not the throne of God in heaven,
but rather the earthly throne predicted by the prophets. It is the
beginning of the fulfillment of Jeremiah's prophecy, "Behold, the
days come, saith the LORD, that I will raise unto David a righteous
Branch, and a King shall reign and prosper, and shall execute judgment and justice in the earth" (Jeremiah 23:5). The place of this
judgment, therefore, is the millennial earth not heaven.

THE SUBJECTS OF THE JUDGMENT

In Matthew 25:32 the subjects of this divine judgment are
clearly declared to be "all nations." The passage could be translated "all Gentiles" as the Greek word is *ethne*. This is a common

word found frequently in the Bible and generally used of non-Jewish races. Although occasionally used of the Jews themselves (cp. Luke 7:5; 23:2; John 11:48, 50, 51, 52; 18:35; Acts 10:22; etc.), the more common meaning is to refer to Gentiles as distinguished from Jews, for instance in the references in Romans 11:13; 15:27; 16:4; Galatians 2:12. In some passages the Gentile character of the word is the main thought as in Romans 3:29; 9:24.

The context here indicates that the nations or the Gentiles should be viewed as the non-Jewish population of the world. In the narrative they are contrasted to "my brethren" (Matthew 25:40) who in the passage are distinguished from both the sheep and the goats, which comprise the entire mass of the Gentiles. In order to maintain the distinctions, it is best to understand it as referring to the non-Jewish peoples of the world. However, a similar judgment awaits the Jewish people (Ezekiel 20:34-38) and the issue is not whether both Jews and Gentiles are judged, but rather whether this passage concerns itself primarily with the Gentiles. In view of the fact that this is the climax of the times of the Gentiles, it seems appropriate that a special judgment should be applied to these who have oppressed Israel throughout their history.

From the English word *nations* some have inferred that what is dealt with here are political entities or countries as such. This is not at all indicated by the word *ethne,* a racial rather than an organizational term, and the details of the prophecy are such that they can be applied only to individuals and not to groups. The expression "all nations" therefore is best understood as referring to all Gentiles and more specifically all Gentiles who are living on earth at this time. It should be understood that many Gentiles at the time of the second coming of Christ were also already judged in the very act of divine wrath being poured on the armies gathered in the Middle East according to Revelation 19:17-21. As this is an earlier event in connection with the second advent, it must be assumed that we have here living Gentiles who were non-combatants or not involved in this great struggle.

THE BASIS OF THE JUDGMENT

This passage in Matthew 25 is a remarkable one in that works are prominent. According to the Scriptures, as all Gentiles are gathered before Christ to be judged they are divided into two classes, one described as "sheep" and the other designated "goats."

According to Matthew 25:33, "he shall set the sheep on his right hand, but the goats on the left." Having made this arbitrary division, He then justifies what He is doing by addressing Himself first to the sheep. In graphic language Christ in His role as "the King" declares to the sheep on his right hand: "Come, ye blessed of my Father, inherit the kingdom prepared for you from the foundation of the world: For I was an hungred, and ye gave me meat: I was thirsty, and ye gave me drink: I was a stranger, and ye took me in: Naked, and ye clothed me: I was sick, and ye visited me: I was in prison, and ye came unto me" (Matthew 25:34-36).

The declaration by Christ is remarkable because attention is called to certain rather ordinary works such as feeding the hungry, giving the thirsty drink, clothing the naked, visiting the sick and those in prison. Furthermore, Christ declares that they who have done these things have done them to Him personally.

The righteous accordingly answer Him with the question, "Lord, when saw we thee an hungred, and fed thee? or thirsty, and gave thee drink? When saw we thee a stranger, and took thee in? or naked, and clothed thee? Or when saw we thee sick, or in prison, and came unto thee?" (Matthew 25:37-39).

In reply Christ as "the King" states, "Verily I say unto you, Inasmuch as ye have done it unto one of the least of these my brethren, ye have done it unto me" (Matthew 25:40).

In contrast to this, Christ then turns to those on the left hand described as goats and declares, "Depart from me, ye cursed, into everlasting fire, prepared for the devil and his angels: For I was an hungred, and ye gave me no meat: I was thirsty, and ye gave me no drink: I was a stranger, and ye took me not in: naked, and ye clothed me not: sick, and in prison, and ye visited me not" (Matthew 25:41-43). In like manner the goats replied asking when they had neglected these works of mercy. The judgment then is pronounced upon the goats by Christ, "Verily I say unto you, Inasmuch as ye did it not to one of the least of these, ye did it not to me. And these shall go away into everlasting punishment: but the righteous into life eternal" (Matthew 25:45, 46).

This passage has troubled expositors for it seems to indicate that the sheep go into life eternal because of their righteous works whereas the wicked are condemned because of their failure to do these prescribed deeds of kindness. The question is naturally raised whether a person can be saved by works. If any passage in the Bible seems to imply it, this would be the passage.

When other Scriptures are brought to bear upon the question of whether people can be saved by works, it soon becomes evident that salvation by works is an impossibility under any circumstances. Although grace may be revealed in different degrees in different dispensations, it is evident from the very doctrine that all men are sinners, that all men are spiritually dead, and that no amount of good works can reverse the sentence of death or change the sinful nature of man. Works can never be the ground of man's salvation. There can be no cure for depravity, Adamic sin, and obvious human failure found in every life, other than the grace of God. Hence, while there may be different dispensations with varying rules of life there can be only one way of salvation, namely, through Christ and His provided redemption. The question remains then how this passage in its plain emphasis on works can be justified.

The answer is first of all found in the fact that in every dispensation works are not the ground of salvation, but rather they are the evidence of salvation. It is always true that "faith without works is dead" (James 2:26). This does not mean that a man is saved by works, but it does mean that one who really trusts God and is the recipient of divine grace will manifest this fact in a changed life. Humanly speaking, it is proper to challenge faith that does not manifest itself in some way. The passage then should be added to all others that emphasize the importance of works, not as the basis for salvation, but as the evidence of it.

A question still remains, however, concerning the precise character of these works. Is it always true that those who are kind to others and feed them and clothe them are necessarily Christians? The obvious philanthropy of many non-Christians in our modern world would seem to indicate that this cannot be taken normally as an indisputable evidence of eternal life.

The answer to the problem is found in the peculiar circumstances which form the background of the judgment. The people who are here being judged as Gentiles are those who have survived the horrors of the great tribulation. In this period which Jeremiah refers to as "the time of Jacob's trouble" (Jeremiah 30:7), anti-semitism will reach an all-time high. It is evident from the warning of Christ in Matthew 24:15-22 that the Jewish people will be hounded to the death especially in the Holy Land, and possibly throughout the world. Satanic hatred will be manifested to a degree never before achieved and will be part of the world-wide satanic deception which will cause men to believe a lie. In the words of II Thessalonians 2:11, "God shall send them strong delusion, that they should believe a lie."

Under these peculiar circumstances, under the strain and stress of satanic hatred of God and compulsion to worship the world ruler, anyone who would befriend a Jew would be a marked man. It is almost inconceivable that one who would be a true worshiper of the beast would ignore the world-wide command to exterminate the Jew. For a Gentile under these circumstances to befriend one who is designated as "my brethren" would be phenomenal and could be motivated only by a realization that the Jewish people are indeed the people of God and that their Messiah is indeed the Saviour of all who believe in Him. A simple work of kindness such as is here described therefore becomes highly significant, and in the context of this judgment one who would perform deeds of kindness would inevitably be a believer in the Lord Jesus Christ. Hence, while the works are not the ground of their salvation, which inevitably must be the grace of God and the sacrifice of Christ, works are nevertheless the evidence of salvation and to this our Lord points.

It is still true that salvation is "not of works, lest any man should boast" (Ephesians 2:9) but rather by faith and by grace.

The importance of works in the final judgments of mankind here has another divine revelation. The sheep who have manifested their faith in Christ under trying circumstances by befriending a Jew are now rewarded by being ushered into the millennial kingdom with its blessings of Christ's righteous rule and beneficent care over all who trust in Him. By contrast, the goats who followed the course of this world and undoubtedly participated in the persecution of the Jewish people as well as neglecting their acts of kindness now come under the divine judgment which they justly deserve, and are cast into everlasting fire.

THE JUDGMENT

The purpose of the judgment of the Gentiles is obviously one of separation of the righteous from the unrighteous in preparation for the millennial kingdom (cp. Matthew 24:40, 41). It is a fulfillment of that which was anticipated in the parables of Matthew

13 where it was predicted that in the end the wheat and the tares would be separated, the good and the bad fish would be dealt with, and the bad fish destroyed. The millennial kingdom will begin with the entire adult population of the world limited to those who have put their trust in Christ. It will be a new beginning comparable to that following the flood when Noah and his immediate family formed the entire population of the earth.

From this context it is also evident that this is not a final judgment of the individuals concerned. Those ushered into the millennial kingdom in this judgment still are in their natural bodies, still have a natural life to live, and ultimately will either die or be translated and have their life reviewed in finality. Although there is no specific revelation of this fact, the general truth of Hebrews 9:27, "as it is appointed unto men once to die, but after this the judgment," it may be concluded that the sheep will be subject to ultimate reward for their works even though at this time they are assured of eternal salvation in that they possess eternal life. In a similar way the casting of the wicked into everlasting fire should not be confused as a final judgment in which they are cast into the lake of fire which does not occur for another thousand years. It is rather that they move into a state of divine judgment described by the word "everlasting fire" such as is true both in Hades, the temporary abode of the wicked dead, and the lake of fire, the final state of the wicked. Their judgment in a word is that they are put to death physically, but subject to future judgment and final resurrection at the Great White Throne judgment. This judgment accordingly ends the times of the Gentiles and begins the millennial rule of Christ.

Chapter XV

THE NATIONS IN THE MILLENNIUM AND
THE ETERNAL STATE

The divine purpose of God for the Gentiles comes to its natural conclusion at the end of the times of the Gentiles which is marked by the second coming of Jesus Christ. The millennial reign of Christ primarily concerns the nation Israel and their restoration to their ancient land. Most of the prophecies dealing with the millennial kingdom describe Israel's day of glory and prominence with Christ as their king and David resurrected from the dead as the prince.

There are, however, numerous prophecies that indicate that the Gentiles also will participate in the millennial reign of Christ and will inherit many of the blessings which characterize this period. As the reign of Christ is from sea to sea it necessarily goes far beyond the borders of the Promised Land, outlined so long ago to Abraham as extending from the River of Egypt to the Euphrates (Genesis 15:18). Outside the Promised Land, but often adjacent to it are the millennial counterparts of the ancient peoples who in one way or another were related to Israel's long history.

EXTENT OF GENTILE PROPHECY

In addition to the major nations which had a large part in the history of Israel such as Babylon, Assyria, and Egypt, a number of important prophecies are found in the Old Testament relating to minor nations. While such prophecies are scattered throughout the Old Testament, three major passages are found in Isaiah 13-23, Jeremiah 46-51, and Ezekiel 25-32. Seven major nations are mentioned in Isaiah to which can be added prophecies concerning the cities of Tyre and Damascus. Jeremiah adds additional prophecies relating to five of these plus a passage on the Ammonites (Jeremiah 49:1-6) and a short prophecy about Kedar and Hazor (49:28-31). Ezekiel offers additional prophecies concerning five

158

of these nations and adds a prophecy about Zidon (Ezekiel 28: 20-24). As special attention has already been directed to the prophecies relating to Babylon, the most prominent nations in these prophecies to be considered here are the remaining nations, namely, Assyria, Egypt, Philistia, Moab, Damascus, Ethiopia, Edom or Dumah, Arabia, the city of Tyre, the Ammonites, Kedar and Hazor, and Zidon.

The great prophecies of Isaiah, Jeremiah, and Ezekiel treat the predictions concerning the nations in the context of Israel's coming day of restoration and glory. Unquestionably the main theme in the prophet's mind, whether it is stated or not, is that Israel in contrast to the nations which surround them is destined for glory and honor in God's ultimate kingdom on earth. This tremendous truth has been blurred by the unfortunate tendency to spiritualize these prophecies in the attempt to make them describe the glory of the church. If they are taken literally, however, they provide a pattern of fulfilled prophecy in the past and a program of unfulfilled prophecy in the future which is tremendously significant in unfolding the great purposes of God for the nations of the world.

The prophet Isaiah for instance portrays the glories of the coming kingdom in Isaiah 11–12 before turning to the prophecies relating to the nations in chapter 13 and following. It is clear that from the prophetic viewpoint the importance of these prophecies relating to the nations can be discovered only in the contrast to the prophecies relating to Israel, many of which are yet unfulfilled.

In a similar way the prophecies of Jeremiah emphasize Israel's restoration and coming glory. Often these prophecies are set in the midst of prophecies relating to the nations and are presented as sharp contrasts to the destined doom of the other nations and God's divine judgment upon them.

The major portion of Jeremiah's section on prophecy concerning the nations occurs late in the book in chapters 46–51 preceded by the historical and prophetical matter describing the stirring relationship of Jeremiah to his contemporary situation coupled with many prophecies concerning Israel in the latter days.

Ezekiel by contrast presents the prophecies concerning the nations first in chapters 25–32 and then follows in chapters 33 and 34 with predictions concerning the coming kingdom. Then after additional prophecies concerning Mount Seir, Israel's future is again depicted in the latter portion of chapter 36. The vision of the valley of dry bones in chapter 37 foreshadows Israel's ultimate restoration. Then before the great section beginning in chapter 40 there are the prophecies concerning Gog and Magog related to Israel's restoration in chapters 38 and 39. It is clear in Ezekiel as in the other prophecies that Israel's future is set into the context of God's dealings with the surrounding nations in the past as well as in the future. A survey of prophecies of these nations can well begin with an examination of prophecy relating to Assyria.

ASSYRIA

The importance of Assyria is borne out by more than 140 references in the Bible to this ancient people and more than 20 references to its principal city Nineveh. First mention is found as early as Genesis 2:14 where Moses in describing the Hiddekel River, later known as the Tigris, stated concerning this river, "that is it which goeth toward the east of Assyria." Moses of course was alluding to Assyria as it existed at the time he was writing Genesis. A similar reference is found in Genesis 25:18.

According to archaeologists, Assyria had a long history. As early as 2900 B.C. colonists, probably from Babylon, settled in a small area between the rivers Tigris and Zab southeast of the Armenian Mountains. Racially they were closely related to the people of Babylonia and mixed with the Sumerian people who were the earlier residents of this area. The Assyrians are generally classified as belonging to the Semitic race. Their language, similar to that of the Babylonians, was written mostly in ideograms on clay and stone by a wedge-shaped instrument, and hence is known as cuneiform.

Assyria first became a great city state under Shamshi-Adad I (1748–1716 B.C.) and increased in power as Babylon declined. Its greatest period, however, began with Tiglath-Pileser I (1114–1076 B.C.) when it extended its borders westward to the Mediterranean Sea and embraced a considerable area. Its power rose and fell for a number of centuries following and it was in this period that Assyria came in contact with Israel. Shalmaneser III (858-824 B.C.) is recorded as fighting Ahab in 853 B.C. and accepted tribute from Jehu, the son of Omri. These incidents, however, are not mentioned in the Bible.

A later ruler, Tiglath-Pileser III, according to II Kings 15:19, conquered Israel and exacted tribute from Menahem and carried off many of the children of Israel as captives. His successor Shalmaneser V (726-722 B.C.) attacked Hoshea of Israel who had revolted against him. His successor, Sargon II (721-705 B.C.), mentioned only in Isaiah 20:1, conquered the capital of Samaria (II Kings 17:3-41). Sennacherib (704-681 B.C.) is recorded as attempting to conquer Jerusalem, but was thwarted by the slaying of his army by the angel of the Lord (II Kings 19:1-37) and was succeeded by his son Esar-haddon. With the rising power of Babylon, Nineveh, capital of Assyria, fell in 612 B.C. under a collation of Babylonian, Median, and Scythian armies. With this event Assyria came abruptly to the end of its career and in a remarkably short time Assyrian civilization was completely destroyed. Its great cities became mounds of debris and for centuries were lost until finally recovered by archaeologists and identified in the nineteenth century.

From the standpoint of prophecy, the history of Assyria is important because along its path numerous prophecies were fulfilled. Isaiah the prophet, for instance, solemnly warned the children of Israel of the coming invasion of the Assyrians and their ultimate captivity (Isaiah 7:17-20; 8:4-7) and predicted that Assyria would be punished in due time and brought down (Isaiah 11:12-16). The entire book of Nahum relates to the downfall of Nineveh, and the book of Jonah records the remarkable experience of repentance of the people of Nineveh at the preaching of Jonah which delayed their ultimate destruction one hundred and fifty years.

Most of the prophecies concerning Nineveh have already been fulfilled. A few references, however, are subject to fulfillment in the millennial reign and events relating to it.

One of the prophecies concerning the destruction of Assyria is found in Micah 5:5, 6 where the context seems to indicate a millennial situation. Some expositors have identified "the Assyrian" of Micah 5:5 as the little horn of Daniel 8 and conclude that the future world ruler who will head the Roman Empire will be an Assyrian. This identification, however, is doubtful, and it is more probable that Micah, living in the period of Assyria's ascendancy, is merely contrasting here the future glory of Israel with the destruction of Nineveh and of Assyria which actually took place in the seventh century B.C.

That Assyria is to be recognized in the millennial situation, however, is indicated in several passages. According to Isaiah 11:

11, 16, the regathering of Israel at the beginning of the millennium will be from Assyria as well as from other nations, and a highway will stretch from Egypt to Assyria through the land of Israel as a major transportation link in the millennial kingdom. A similar prophecy is found in Isaiah 19:23-25 in reference to the future millennial kingdom: "In that day shall there be a highway out of Egypt to Assyria, and the Assyrian shall come into Egypt, and the Egyptian into Assyria, and the Egyptians shall serve with the Assyrians. In that day shall Israel be the third with Egypt and with Assyria, even a blessing in the midst of the land: Whom the LORD of hosts shall bless, saying, Blessed be Egypt my people, and Assyria the work of my hands, and Israel mine inheritance."

It is evident from this passage that Israel's two most important neighbors in the millennial kingdom will be the peoples who inhabit the area of ancient Assyria to the northeast and Egypt to the southwest. In that day both Assyria and Egypt will be blessed along with Israel. The fact that Israel is called "third" in the light of other prophecies should not be interpreted, however, as meaning that Israel is less than these nations, but rather that it will be spoken of in the same breath as a prominent world power of that day. Another reference to Israel's regathering from Assyria is found in Isaiah 27:13. Zechariah adds his contribution in Zechariah 10:10, 11 where the destruction of the pride of Assyria and the scepter of Egypt is predicted and the regathering of Israel from these lands is anticipated. Assyria, the great nation of the past which antedated the Babylonian Empire and successive dominions of the Gentiles, will have its echo in the prophetic future and its place in the divine program of the millennial kingdom.

EGYPT

In the millennial situation, Egypt likewise is to have a prominent place as already illustrated in passages cited concerning Assyria. Israel will be regathered from Egypt to their Promised Land, but Egypt will be a prominent nation in the millennial situation. That Egypt will be blessed is mentioned specifically in Isaiah 19:25 and that it will be a prominent nation along with Israel and Assyria is indicated in the same passage. Egypt is singled out for special warning in Zechariah 14:18, 19; God will punish them unless they keep the feast of tabernacles in the millennial kingdom. What is revealed in respect to Egypt has reference to the world-wide rule of Christ and indicates that all people will necessarily be required to serve Him.

PHILISTIA

The prominence of the Philistines in the history of Israel is demonstrated by approximately 270 references to them in the Old Testament. Most of these concern historic events depicting the constant struggle between Israel and the Philistines. A few references to the Philistines contain prophecies of their doom or defeat at the hands of Israel already fulfilled. References such as Jeremiah 47:1; Ezekiel 25:15, 16; Amos 1:8; Zephaniah 2:5; and Zechariah 9:6 are probably best interpreted as already fulfilled.

A few references to the Philistines, however, are found in a context of the future millennial kingdom and imply that the territory of the Philistines and the inhabitants in that future day will have a relationship to the kingdom. According to Isaiah 11:14 Israel will have domination over the Philistines in that day. Again in Obadiah 19 the house of Jacob shall possess the Philistines. In both of these prophecies it may be presumed that the writer of Scripture is referring to the territory known to them at that time as possessed by the Philistines and to the future inhabitants of that area. It means simply that Israel will be victorious over their ancient enemies and possess their territory.

MOAB

Of the more than 180 references to Moab in the Old Testament, the great majority deal with historic events. They had many contacts with the children of Israel during the Exodus as well as in the period of the judges. The fact that Ruth was a Moabitess and in the lineage of David sets this people apart.

The first important prophetic utterance relative to Moab is recorded in Numbers 24:17 where Balaam predicted concerning the Messiah, "I shall see him, but not now: I shall behold him, but not nigh: there shall come a Star out of Jacob, and a Sceptre shall rise out of Israel, and shall smite the corners of Moab, and destroy all the children of Sheth." The reference is, of course, to the Davidic line of which Christ is the ultimate fulfillment, and the prophecy anticipates not only the conquering of the Moabites under David and his successors but the ultimate possession of the land by Israel in the coming kingdom.

In Isaiah 11:14 a similar reference is found where the children of Israel are predicted to conquer Edom and Moab as well as the Philistines and the children of Ammon. This too refers to the possession of the land by Israel in the millennial kingdom.

Still another allusion to the Moabites in the future is included in the prophecies of the final world war described in Daniel 11: 40-45. In Daniel 11:41 Moab along with Edom and the children of Ammon is said to escape the warfare between the king of the north and the king of the south with the Roman world ruler. This will have its fulfillment in the days just preceding the second coming of Christ.

The more extensive prophecies relating to Moab seem to have their primary fulfillment in history. These prophecies anticipate that Moab will be punished by God for their sins and for their opposition to the children of Israel. Some of them, like Isaiah 25:10, may have a future reference like those previously considered and will be fulfilled in the millennial kingdom. But the great prophetic passages such as Isaiah 15:1–16:14, Jeremiah 48:1-47, and Ezekiel 25:8-11, although describing in detail the downfall of Moab, seem to have their primary fulfillment in events of the past. Although they may foreshadow, as prophecy often does, the ultimate triumph of the children of Israel, the two important prophetic references to Moab in the minor prophets, namely Amos 2:1, 2 and Zephaniah 2:8, 9, refer to judgments already fulfilled.

Although the unfulfilled prophecies relating to Moab do not seem to be a large proportion of the total material provided in Scripture, they add their evidence to the total picture of the future kingdom in which Israel will be restored and triumphant over her traditional enemies.

DAMASCUS

Damascus was one of the most ancient cities of the Middle East and one of the few to have a continuous history down to modern times. First mentioned in Genesis 14:15, it continued to have a relationship to Israel throughout the Old Testament period where there are more than forty references and in the New Testament where it is mentioned fifteen times. The more extended prophecies as found in Isaiah 17:1-14 and Jeremiah 49:23-27 have all been fulfilled as well as the occasional references found in Isaiah 7:8; 8:4; Amos 1:3-5; 3:12; 5:27. In Ezekiel 47:16-18 and 48:1 reference is made to Damascus as being in existence in the coming kingdom and furnishing identification for the borders of the land of Israel. No events are predicted and the reference seems to be to geography rather than to people who inhabit the land at that time. It is of interest that Damascus, which has had such a long history, apparently will continue its existence into the millennial kingdom.

THE ETHIOPIANS

The Ethiopians were so named by the Greeks and the Romans and refer to those known as the children of Cush in the Hebrew. They were descendants of Ham and occupied the area south of Egypt. Although most of the references to Ethiopians seem to concern events already fulfilled or historic in connection with the Ethiopians, some of the statements seem to be prophetic. The extended prophecy of Isaiah 18:1-7, while largely fulfilled, seems to go beyond the past, such as in the prediction of Isaiah 18:7 where it is stated that the Ethiopians shall be brought as a subdued people to the Lord of hosts in Mount Zion. Isaiah 45:14 may also be interpreted as picturing the triumph of Israel over the Ethiopians in the kingdom period, although the reference may be to historic fulfillment. The predictions of Isaiah 20:3-5 and 43:3 seem to have had adequate fulfillment in the past. The prophecies of Ezekiel 30:4, 5 relating as they do to the Day of the Lord may well have some future fulfillment. The reference to Ethiopia in Ezekiel 38:5, because it describes a northern invasion, has been taken by some to refer to another people, but in any event it is future and a part of the great northern invasion of Israel yet to be fulfilled.

Several other future references to Ethiopia seem to be found in the prophets. In Daniel 11:43 Ethiopia is mentioned as one of the countries that escaped warfare in the final world struggle which apparently reaches Egypt, but does not go farther south. In Psalm 68:31 it is predicted, "Ethiopia shall soon stretch out her hands unto God." This seemingly refers to the future millennial kingdom, although the prophecy of Zephaniah 2:12 of destruction at the hands of the Lord probably was fulfilled in the past. The prediction of Zephaniah 3:10, that the Ethiopians will come as suppliants to the Lord, fits best into the future millennial kingdom.

Taken as a whole, the references to Ethiopia recognize their continued significance in God's program and their ultimate destiny as one of the Gentile nations which will be subordinate to Israel when Christ reigns on earth.

EDOM

The descendants of Esau are frequently mentioned in the Old Testament under various designations, but usually as the Edomites. Many of the prophecies relating to Edom have already been fulfilled, such as the extended predictions of Jeremiah 9:26; 25:21; 49:7-22; Lamentations 4:22; Ezekiel 25:12-14; Joel 3:19; Amos 1:6, 9, 11; 2:1. Some of these may be a foreshadowing of ultimate subjugation of Edom in the millennial kingdom.

The prophecies concerning Esau and his descendants stem from the original prophecy of Isaac. After Jacob had stolen the blessing intended for Esau, Isaac pronounced the lesser blessing on Esau recorded in Genesis 27:39, 40. Esau is promised physical blessing, but is put under the dominion of Jacob, although it is predicted that he would break the yoke of Jacob from off his neck. The long history of the relationship of the children of Jacob to the descendants of Esau carried out the conflict anticipated here and the children of Edom continued to figure in prophecy up to and including the kingdom age.

Isaiah 11:14 mentions Edom as being subdued by Israel in the kingdom period. Isaiah 63:1 is a prophetic description of the coming of Christ in judgment at His second coming. He is described as coming "from Edom." Daniel 11:41 includes Edom as one of the countries which escape warfare in the final world conflict before the second coming.

The most extended prophecy concerning Edom is found in Obadiah which is entirely devoted to this subject. Verses 1 to 14 speak of the judgment of God upon Edom because of their sins in rejoicing over the captivity of the children of Judah. These prophecies had at least partial fulfillment. The passage, verses 15-21, which conclude the book, picture Edom in the Day of the Lord as having experienced divine judgment and being under the domination of the house of Jacob. The age-long controversy between Esau and Jacob will be resolved in Jacob's favor in keeping with the sovereign choice of God in which it was declared that the elder should serve the younger (Romans 9:12). Taken as a whole, the prophecies relating to Edom have already had amazing fulfillment in so far as God's judgment has fallen upon them in the past. The ultimate fulfillment awaits the second coming of Christ.

ARABIA

Of the comparatively few references to Arabia in the Bible, the principal prophecy is found in Isaiah 21:13-17. Although the passage is not entirely clear, it seems to have been already fulfilled in the past. The kings of Arabia are also mentioned as those who will drink of the divine judgment of God in Jeremiah 25:24, probably already fulfilled. In Isaiah 13:20 it is also mentioned that the Arabian will no longer pitch his tent in Babylon after its destruction. On the whole, these prophecies are brief and insignificant in the total program of God.

TYRE

The city of Tyre like Damascus is one of the ancient cities of the world. Its riches and commercial interests were renowned, and it figured largely in the history of the ancient world. Although assigned to the tribe of Asshur, it was not subdued by them, but through much of its history was in friendly relationship with Israel as during the time of the reign of Solomon. Because of a fortress on an island in the Mediterranean to which the people could retire when Tyre was under siege, Tyre was very difficult to subdue and was able to resist the Assyrian armies and stand off Nebuchadnezzar the king of Babylon for more than a dozen years. Alexander the Great had to construct a causeway from the mainland in order to conquer it, and in the process fulfilled many of the prophecies concerning the destruction of the city itself.

Most of the prophecies concerning Tyre have already been fulfilled, such as Isaiah 23:1-18; Jeremiah 25:22; 47:4; Joel 3:4-8; Amos 1:9, 10, and Zechariah 9:2-4.

The importance of Tyre prophetically stems largely from the great prophecy of Ezekiel where three long chapters are devoted to Tyre, namely, 26, 27, and 28. Chapter 26 of Ezekiel describes the judgment which is impending upon Tyre. The immediate occasion was Nebuchadnezzar's siege of the city, but it goes beyond the immediate situation to its ultimate destruction later at the hands of Alexander the Great. Then the remarkable prophecy of Ezekiel 26:14 was fulfilled which reads: "And I will make thee like the top of a rock: thou shalt be a place to spread nets upon; thou shalt be built no more: for I the LORD have spoken it, saith the Lord GOD." The city of Tyre was literally scraped to the rock in order to provide materials to build a causeway out to its island fortress. Visitors to Tyre today can see the evidence of this fulfillment.

Chapter 27 of Ezekiel is a long lamentation over the destruction of Tyre with its description of the riches which once characterized this city. The lamentation is extended to the prince of Tyre in Ezekiel 28:1-10. The prophecies to this point can probably best be interpreted as having been graphically fulfilled in the long history of Tyre.

The prophetic utterance of Ezekiel 28:12-15, while having a partial reference to Tyre, seems to go beyond the immediate human ruler to Satan himself in his original conflict with God. He is described as "the anointed cherub that covereth" who at one time was "perfect . . . from the day that thou wast created, till iniquity was found in thee." Many interpreters from Augustine to modern times have felt that this description is a revelation of the character of the original rebellion of Satan against God when he, according to the parallel description in Isaiah 14:12-15, sought to be like God and take the place of God in worship. The Ezekiel passage, however, beginning in verse 16 seems to return largely to a description of Tyre itself and predicts its utter destruction. The large place afforded Tyre in these three long chapters of Ezekiel indicate its importance from the prophetic standpoint as not only embodying divine judgment upon a wicked city which had exalted itself above God, but also upon its unseen ruler, Satan. The entire prophecy anticipates the downfall of Satan as well as the city of Tyre itself. As far as the prophetic program of God is concerned, Tyre does not seem to figure largely in end-time events, although the intimation is that it will be in existence in some form as a city in the time of the end.

MISCELLANEOUS PROPHECIES

Among the lesser prophecies concerning the nations is that concerning the Ammonites. Although the Ammonites are mentioned frequently in the Bible, they do not loom large in the prophetic narrative. One of the major passages is found in Jeremiah 49:1-6 where God's divine judgment and conquest of the Ammonites is pictured. A similar passage is found in Ezekiel 25:1-7 which prophesies the conquest of the Ammonites by "the men of the east." Other references to the Ammonites in prophecy now fulfilled are passages such as Jeremiah 25:21; Amos 1:13; and Zephaniah 2:8, 9.

The only reference clearly future is that of Daniel 11:41 where Ammon is said to escape some of the warfare at the end of the age. The dealings of God with the children of Ammon again illustrate His justice and the certainty of fulfilled prophecy.

A brief prophecy concerning Kedar and Hazor is contained in Jeremiah 49:28-33. It is a prediction of judgment upon them at the hands of Nebuchadnezzar king of Babylon. A similar judgment is pronounced upon Elam in Jeremiah 49:34-38. Other references to God's judgment on Kedar are found in Isaiah 21:16, 17. Only future reference relative to those of Kedar seems to be found in Isaiah 60:7 where it is indicated that "the flocks of Kedar shall be gathered together" as possessions of the coming Messiah.

Mention should also be made of Zidon also spelled Sidon, another ancient city on the eastern Mediterranean north of Tyre. In Ezekiel 28:20-24 it is predicted that Zidon will be subject to divine judgment of pestilence and warfare because of their sins. This has unquestionably been fulfilled already in history. Zidon is also mentioned as participating in the general judgment which falls upon Tyre in Isaiah 23:2, 4, 12 and is also associated with Tyre in other prophecies, such as Jeremiah 25:22; 47:4, and Joel 3:4. As a city it does not figure largely in prophecy.

A survey of the countries surrounding Israel demonstrate that prophecies of their coming judgment and subjugation to Israel are set in a context of Israel's exaltation in the kingdom age. Although in some cases the reference may be largely geographic rather than to the nations themselves, for racial continuity may be difficult to sustain, the language of Scripture is sufficiently clear to make plain that Israel will triumph over her enemies and in the process be restored to a place of glory and blessing under the rule of the Messiah. The fact that Israel is already in her place in the Middle East is a foreshadowing of these ultimate triumphs which await the second coming of her Messiah and Saviour.

THE NATIONS IN THE ETERNAL STATE

It is only natural that prophecies relating to the nations should be primarily concerned with the present earth rather than the eternal state. It is an error, however, to assume that national identity will be lost in eternity. Just as there will be individual identity, so also there will be racial identity, and individuals will inevitably carry throughout eternity an identification related to some extent to their place in the history of the world. Hence, Israelites will be Israelites throughout eternity and Gentiles will be Gentiles as well.

Although there has been some resistance to this idea, national identity seems a natural corollary to individual identity. If Abraham is to remain Abraham throughout eternity and David is to remain David, it is inevitable that they would be considered in their historical context in time. So also will it be with those who are saved among the Gentiles. There is no indication that nationality of individuals will be stressed, but the fact that they belong to a nation is revealed in the description of the New Jerusalem.

According to the revelation given to John, the New Jerusalem will include the angels (Revelation 21:12), the children of Israel (Revelation 21:12), the church as represented in the twelve apostles (Revelation 21:14) and the Gentiles (Revelation 21:24). This is anticipated in the itemization of those who will be related to the heavenly Jerusalem given in Hebrews 12:22, 23 where specifically the heavenly Jerusalem includes "an innumerable company of angels," the "church of the firstborn," and "the spirits of just men made perfect." This latter reference seems to be an inclusive one referring to all men who are saved who are not included in the previous itemization. Such a description obviously includes Gentiles who were saved. Hence, the reference to "the nations," better translated "the Gentiles," in Revelation 21:24 is not surprising.

Expositors are of course disagreed as to whether this description relates to the heavenly city in the millennial period or in the eternal state. In either case, however, the implication is that the same people who inhabit the eternal city in this description will continue to inhabit it throughout eternity. The conclusion is therefore sound and valid that the saved among the Gentiles will find their place in the eternal bliss which will characterize the saints in eternity to come as they dwell in perfect fellowship with God in the heavenly city, the New Jerusalem.

Although the pattern of Gentile prophecy and fulfillment is largely one of judgment upon their unbelief and blasphemous rebellion against God, it is another token of the grace of God that, in addition to His program for Israel and the church, the body of Christ, countless Gentiles in the Old Testament period as well as in the tribulation and the millennium will come to know Jesus Christ and His saving grace, and accordingly will be qualified to participate as individuals in the blessings which God has ordained for those who love Him. The majestic purpose of God for the nations is therefore crowned with this happy note of the triumph of grace in those among the Gentiles who turn to Jesus Christ.

Taken as a whole, the program of God for the Gentiles emphasizes His righteousness and His sovereignty which, though challenged for many centuries, ultimately has its clear declaration at the second coming of Jesus Christ. Throughout eternity, however, the presence of Gentiles who entered the eternal state is the reminder of the comprehensive character of the grace of God which provided Jesus Christ as a means of reconciling the world unto Himself. Their testimony will join with that of all other saints and the holy angels in the mighty symphony of worship and praise which will constitute the music of eternity.

CHAPTER XVI

AMERICA IN PROPHECY

One of the natural questions facing the world, but especially citizens of the United States of America, is the place of the United States in the unfulfilled prophetic program. In the last fifty years, the United States of America has become one of the most powerful and influential nations of all history. What does the Bible contribute to the question of the future of the United States?

In keeping with the principle that prophecy is primarily concerned with the Holy Land and its immediate neighbors, it is not surprising that geographic areas remote from this center of Biblical interest should not figure largely in prophecy and may not be mentioned at all. No specific mention of the United States or any other country in North America or South America can be found in the Bible. None of the rather obscure references to distant lands can be taken specifically as a reference to the United States. Any final answer to the question is therefore an impossibility, but nevertheless some conclusions of a general character can be reached.

The World Situation at the End Time

As previous study of prophecy has indicated, the Scriptures provide an outline of major events in the period beginning with the rapture of the church and ending with the second coming of Christ to establish His kingdom. Immediately after the rapture there will be a period of preparation in which the ten-nation confederacy in the Mediterranean will emerge and the little horn of Daniel 7 will be revealed as its eventual dictator. At the same time there will be the emergence of a world church as suggested in Revelation 17.

At the conclusion of this period of preparation the head of the Mediterranean confederacy, who will be the Roman "prince that shall come," will make a covenant with Israel (Daniel 9:27) which will introduce the second phase of the period, namely, a

172

period of protection and peace for Israel. After enduring for three and a half years or one half of the projected seven-year period contemplated in the covenant, the Roman ruler will take the role of world dictator, assume the prerogatives of deity, and begin the great tribulation with its corresponding period of persecution for Israel and the emergence of a world religion with the world ruler as its deity. This third period will be climaxed by the second coming of Christ to the earth and its attending judgments.

THE RELATION OF THE UNITED STATES TO THESE WORLD EVENTS

Although the Scriptures do not give any clear word concerning the role of the United States in relationship to the revived Roman Empire and the later development of the world empire, it is probable that the United States will be in some form of alliance with the Roman ruler. Most citizens of the United States of America have come from Europe and their sympathies would be more naturally with a European alliance than with Russia or countries in Eastern Asia. It may even be that the United States will provide large support for the Mediterranean confederacy as it seems to be in opposition to Russia, Eastern Asia, and Africa. Actually a balance of power in the world may exist at that time not too dissimilar to the present world situation, namely, that Europe and the Mediterranean area will be in alliance with America in opposition to Russia, Eastern Asia, and Africa. Based on geographic, religious and economic factors such an alliance of powers seems a natural sequence of present situations in the world.

If the end-time events include a destruction of Russia and her allies prior to the final period of great tribulation, this may trigger an unbalance in the world situation that will permit the Roman ruler to become a world ruler. In this event, it should be clear that the United States will be in a subordinate role and no longer the great international power that it is today.

It has been suggested by some that the total absence of Scriptural comment on the United States of America in the end time is evidence that the United States previously has been destroyed by an atomic war or some other catastrophic means and therefore no longer is a voice in international affairs. Such a solution, however, overlooks the fact that not only the United States but all of the Americas are omitted from prophecy, and the same is true of

Australia. The fact is there are few references to any country at some distance from the Holy Land. The view, therefore, would be preferable that while the United States is in existence and possibly a power to be reckoned with in the rapidly moving events which characterize the end of the age, world political power will be centered in the Mediterranean area and necessarily the United States will play a subordinate role.

History has many records of great nations which have risen to unusual power and influence only to decline because of internal corruption or international complications. It may well be that the United States of America is today at the zenith of its power much as Babylon was in the sixth century B.C. prior to its sudden downfall at the hands of the Medes and the Persians (Daniel 5). Any realistic survey of moral conditions in the world today would justify a judgment of God on any nation, including that of the United States. The longsuffering God has offered unusual benefits to the United States both in a material and religious way, but they have been used with such profligacy that ultimate divine judgment may be expected. The question no longer is whether America deserves judgment, but rather why divine judgment has been so long withheld from a nation which has enjoyed so much of God's bounty.

A partial answer may be found in the fact that the United States of America in spite of its failures has nevertheless been a source of major Christian testimony in the world and has done more to promote the missionary cause in terms of money and men than any other nation. Although the United States numbers only five per cent of the total world population, in the last century probably more than fifty per cent of the missionaries and money spent has come from America. In view of the fact that it is God's major purpose in this present age to call out Jew and Gentile to faith in Christ and to have the Gospel preached in all nations, the prosperity which has been true of America has made possible this end and may have been permitted by God to accomplish His holy purposes.

Another important reason for delay in divine judgment upon America is the Abrahamic promise concerning his seed, "I will bless them that bless thee, and curse him that curseth thee" (Genesis 12:3). The United States for the most part has been kind to the Jew. Here the seed of Abraham has had religious freedom and opportunity to make wealth. Judgment on other nations has frequently been preceded by persecution of the Jew. So far in the United States the Jew has had equal treatment.

It is evident, however, that if Christ came for His church and all true Christians were caught out of this world, America then would be reduced to the same situation as other countries. The true church will be gone, and Israel may be persecuted. The drastically changed situation would no longer call for material or political blessing upon the United States. It would therefore follow that with the removal of the principal cause for withholding judgment, namely, the promotion of the missionary cause and befriending the wandering Jew, reason would no longer exist for maintaining America in its present standard of power politically and economically. It may well be that the United States, like Babylon of old, will lose its place of leadership in the world, and this will be a major cause in the shift of power to the Mediterranean scene.

CONCLUSION

Although conclusions concerning the role of America in prophecy in the end time are necessarily tentative, the Scriptural evidence is sufficient to conclude that America in that day will not be a major power and apparently does not figure largely in either the political, economic, or religious aspects of the world. America may well be at its zenith today both in power, influence, and opportunity. In view of the imminent return of the Lord, the time is short and the cause of evangelism is urgent. If prophecy has any one message as bearing on our times, it is that time and opportunity are short, and impending world conditions soon may close the door for further witness in many areas. What is true of America is true for the evangelical church throughout the world, and prophecy in general serves to emphasize the importance of the present task of bearing witness to the Gospel, beginning at Jerusalem and to the uttermost parts of the world.

The destiny of nations is in the hands of the omnipotent God. History is moving inexorably to its prophesied consummation. The divine program in all its detail will be fulfilled. The Son of God will reign in Zion. The nations will bow at His feet. Ultimately the present earth will be replaced with a new heaven and a new earth in which the New Jerusalem will be the home of the redeemed of all ages. All nations will continue throughout eternity to worship and adore the infinite Triune God whose majesty, wisdom, and power will be unquestioned. In that eternal day, God's love and grace will be supremely revealed in those among all nations who are redeemed by the blood of the Lamb.

Date